YOUR WEDDING, YOUR WAY

A Guide to Contemporary Wedding Options

Your Wedding, Your Way

A GUIDE TO CONTEMPORARY WEDDING OPTIONS

By CAROL NEWMAN

DOUBLEDAY & COMPANY, INC.
GARDEN CITY, NEW YORK

Library of Congress Cataloging in Publication Data

Newman, Carol.
Your wedding, your way.

1. Wedding etiquette. I. Title.
BJ2051.N43   395'.22
ISBN 0-385-09608-9
Library of Congress Catalog Card Number 74-18821

For
ISABELLE M. TRAINER
(1916–1972)
who was a magnificent woman

CONTENTS

"New modes of communal celebration are emerging. Not that the old ones were bad, but that every so often a generation must say things in new ways, with new languages, new forms . . . else the vital impulse of man dies aborning—smothered by the once good which would substitute its product for the living process."

ROSS SNYDER
Contemporary Celebration

AUTHOR'S NOTE

The book you are reading came into being because my husband and I wanted to get married without inviting the commercialism of the bridal industry. Nor did we want a "correct" wedding bound up by tenets of etiquette that meant nothing to us. We didn't want a mighty bash with expensive meals, bands, and extras, though we did want to celebrate. A civil ceremony seemed deadly. And we thought a "far-out, superheavy" wedding, an antiwedding almost, was not the point we wanted to make. There had to be something that was "just us." A statement somewhere between a cathedral train and blue jeans.

Your Wedding, Your Way is aimed at young people in their twenties and early thirties. Like my husband and me, and the majority of our friends, this nationwide strata of the population has made an attempt to express themselves freely. Most of us, having already gone through a period of rejecting all traditional values and established views, are now trying to weed out the "significants" in our lives. We all are on different levels of consciousness. Some of us are working our way through life using patterns that our parents would not find dissimilar. Others are still bucking their backgrounds. On the subject of weddings we have reached an agreement:

A wedding is a social celebration where two people can make a personalized statement about their love and their desire for recognized unity. A wedding is not to be bulldozed by outdated etiquette or threatened by prohibitive costs.

None of the suggestions or options in *Your Wedding, Your Way* are operable if they are not right for you. This book should have no more authoritative rights over your wedding than a book of etiquette, a bridal consultant, or the mother of the bride. Offered here are ideas and suggestions, occasionally peppered with strong opinions. If they don't coincide with your opinions, then they don't count.

Sometimes it's difficult to know what you really want. The more a couple strives toward individualization in their wedding, the more stressful the new freedom can become. But individualization is important. How you handle your wedding makes a statement about yourself: who you are, how you see yourself, where you're going. As a joint effort it's a good indication of your joint approach to life.

Following are some guidelines that you can use to evaluate your wedding plans in terms of what is most right for you:

1. Do your plans reflect your values and tastes?
   Have you been too heavily influenced by parents, fads, or wedding etiquette rules.

2. Are your plans authentic?
   Are you ruling out ideas that are silly, trite, or unimportant to your statement of love? Does the symbolism involved say exactly what you mean?

3. Do your plans represent the combined ideas and efforts of both of you?

4. Are your plans economically realistic?

Doing what is most right for you is the premise of this book.

Another premise—this book is addressed to the second-person plural. The "you" in these pages generally refers to you as a couple. While most books on weddings are addressed to brides, *Your Wedding, Your Way* assumes that there are two people designing and carrying out the wedding plans—a man and a woman who want to be married.

Your Wedding, Your Way also assumes that, for the most

part, you already know what the standard operating procedures of a traditional wedding are and that you have found those procedures wanting or too expensive. In going through the specific chapters of this book you'll find out how traditional wedding procedures can be personalized, or modified, and how costs can be cut at all levels. The book will also suggest original styles and alternative procedures to be used in place of the traditional. It will attempt to offer guidelines for planning and executing a personalized ceremony.

1. INTRODUCTION

One definition of culture is that it is a system of expectations. People are comfortable when they know what to expect. If there is a right way and a wrong way to go about something, society can proceed with its functionings and sanctionings with certain predetermined points of reference. Things are kept under control. Stability reigns.

All of us require a framework of some kind. We need some gauge of what actions are appropriate. But in today's multicolored society, our framework supports an amazing range of possibilities—all within the realm of reason. We are gaining more and more leeway in our interactions with other people. Today, people who need straight-and-narrow rules to keep "from doing the wrong thing" are considered "uptight."

Even so, something strange happens when it comes time to organize a wedding. Everyone suddenly becomes very conscious of THE RULES. Even freethinkers who have been running their own lives for a long, successful period of time suddenly start to worry about exact wording, proper seating —minuscule details that would make them furious and embarrassed under normal conditions.

Of course, people don't give themselves a wedding every year (usually). There is a "special occasion" element that calls for a marked difference from normal behavior. Yet, it is because of that very element of uniqueness that a wedding should be personalized to fit the participants. Given that a wedding will not occur often in one's life and that it is a ceremony which makes a very personal statement, it seems thoughtless to rely on rules of etiquette and blanket traditions to make the occasion meaningful.

People who rush for the rule books to insure that their wedding will be carried out "correctly" wind up with a specific format. That one format cannot be expected to express what all couples want to say about their love, their union, and themselves. It's very sad that the most personal of all life's celebrations can be robbed of its intensity by formulas and sets of dated rules.

The defenders of rules and traditions have an argument that goes something like this: In this world of changing values, tradition means more now than ever before.

Which, in part, is true. A tradition used in a wedding celebration can be lovely and important. But only if the particular tradition applies to you. Embracing traditions that are not a statement of yourselves is an act of insecurity, an unwillingness to define what is significant in your own lives.

By that same reasoning, vehement rejection of all tradition and established views is ridiculous and represents just as much insecurity. People who cannot abide custom because it is custom are still trying to prove something to the world.

The above examines tradition in rather philosophical terms, but there is a flip side to the issue. Wedding traditions are also big business. Suppliers to the bride make up one of the more commercial and lucrative industries in the United States.

At recent count, the bridal industry was taking in $7.2 billion a year. To promote this volume of business, the industry heavily advertises the status-symbol overtones of a wedding. Particularly affected are the middle-class or working-class families who consider caterers and engraved notices their temporary break-through into the upper crust. A formal wedding is, after all, a collection of the upper- and upper-middle-class social modes. Families who don't ordinarily live Emily Post lives still feel obliged—and actually honored—to follow an etiquette-book wedding. They are often the families who can least afford it. There have been many daughters who took lifetime savings, pensions, loans, and second mortgages down the bridal path on that "day of days."

There is no doubt about it. Wedding etiquette in the United States is tied up in dollar signs by the bridal industry. If you ever doubt it, notice how quickly a supplier to the wedding market will whip out rules on the "proper" way to do this or that. The etiquette books back up the suppliers' businesses. No wonder they would like to see their dictates graven in stone.

Historically, the wedding has always been more human than spiritual, and finances were often involved—starting with the cost of buying a bride. To some extent, weddings, with all their pomp and accessories, have traditionally been used to display the wealth and good taste of the bride's, or groom's, family. But the showmanship and money poured into weddings can get out of hand. Many parents of today's marriageable couples had small, unsophisticated, often quick ceremonies during World War II or the Korean War. The combination of a deprived past and new-found money makes such parents easy game for the heart-tuggers of the bridal industry.

Given the right amount of money, the bridal biz can make any wedding into an "unforgettable" occasion. First, the engraver, bridal-dress shop, and florist take whatever they can get away with. ("Seventy-five dollars might *seem* like a lot for a veil, but you'll only ever have one wedding and you'll look like such a lovely bride. . . .") From matchbooks and napkins, printed with the couple's names, to $60 bridal bouquets ("You really should have two of them, Mrs. Baumgarten— one for her bridal portrait the week before . . ."), to the white aisle runner which now can be dyed to match the bridesmaids' frocks, it's all a maddening round of "fleece the bride's father," and it's made possible by emotional sabotage.

Not only is father faced with giving his little girl "the big-

gest day of her life," he moreover is inviting his friends, relatives, business associates, and prospective in-laws as witnesses
to his largess. Dad is being pressured into making this good.

Then comes the big hook—the reception. Caterers and
banquet-hall managers are doing a turnaway business with
men like Dad. Large cash deposits must be left as long as a
year in advance. Sometimes the deposit is simply absorbed
as a gratuity.

The basic sit-down dinner today can run $15 a head for
the meal alone. The extras—such as lace tablecloths, Florentine candlesticks, an open bar, special desserts, a dove centerpiece—can jack up the tab to $30 a head and higher. And it's
the extras that tug at prewedding anxieties. It's the extras
that will make the wedding memorable and will wow the
friends and relatives.

Long Island, New York, has seen the rise of the "wedding
palace"—the highest order of bridal-reception overkill. The
three most popular palaces are huge banquet establishments
which can accommodate four or five weddings at a time.
Favorite décor is Louis XIV with pastel brocade, padded up-
holstery, garnished mirrors, cupid statues, fountains, and gold
leaf on everything. One establishment has a two-story water-
fall. Nearby is a thirty-foot crystal chandelier that cost $50,-
000 and was modeled after a similar giant in an Austrian
castle.

An important part of the wedding palace is the powder
room. According to the manager, every mother of the bride
asks to see the powder room in advance of booking. He is
proud that great pains have been taken so the powder room
will "knock 'em dead."

Most palaces have a chapel and one has three chapels—
one for each faith. The chapels are a convenience used by
many customers so that the ceremony itself need not be held
too far from the reception—the main event of the day.

After the ceremony, the bride hides away in one of the

ultrafeminine boudoirs until the guests have swept down a buffet table of hors d'oeuvres. Then it's time for the bride to make her grand entrance. The wedding palace upholds the philosophy that the bride should be a star—a queen for the day. Each palace provides their stars with a variety of ways to make a dramatic and queenly entrance.

One of the more lavish banquet halls faces a revolving stage copied after the Metropolitan Opera's *Lohengrin* set. The bride seems to appear out of nowhere in a fine mist. She is positioned on a slowly revolving turntable on top of the stage so that awed wedding guests can admire her from all angles. After the ooh's and ah's die down the four-course dinner proceeds. (If the meal is over a certain price per head, the waiters will serve in white gloves.)

Most wedding-palace affairs total between $2,000 and $5,000. Occasionally, the happy occasion prices itself up into the $10,000 to $20,000 range. Band, flowers, photos, and favors are extra, of course.

If the parents of the bride are being raked over, the bride herself is being pressured by sources old and new. The first mistake she often makes is to buy the latest issue of a bridal magazine. These magazines are amazing periodicals. They are chocked full of gorgeous four-color advertising and contain almost no editorial copy except for random articles which are, for the most part, consumer related. The "Pre-wedding Schedule" and "Who Pays for What" lists are published over and over again in consecutive issues. Sometimes the artwork isn't even changed. Big new ads, but the same editorial content as the previous issue.

To follow through with the advertising, manufacturers of bridal merchandise and household goods have invented soft-sell specialists to urge on the aspiring bride. These specialists are known as "consultants" and there's a consultant for every item a bride should want.

There is the bridal-shop consultant, the gift-registry con-

sultant, the home-planning consultant, and the groom's
consultant. It's enough to make a levelheaded couple forego
the whole idea of a wedding and quietly run away (or continue) to live in sin.

The bridal magazines promote wantsmanship and a commercial view of life. How can they be seriously offered to the
young woman of America? Because not only is the "bride-to-
be" a conditioned consumer, she is being sabotaged by her
upbringing. Since the age of five or six she has treasured an
image of herself as a bride dressed in flowing white. This
image is installed free-of-charge in the heads of all girl children. When she is of age, the pay-off comes. The once-in-a-
lifetime occasion. The consultants, like evil fairies, are there
to collect their dues.

Planning and financing a wedding is a three-way stretch for
those being married for the first time. You are expected to
stage a "perfect" wedding ceremony, acquire all the accou-
terments of a home—right down to the electric corn popper
—and immediately after the ceremony embark on a major
vacation. For some reason, the majority of brides, grooms,
and their families think it is entirely reasonable to take on
these three major expenditures at once. As one aware groom
complained, "There seems to be a mentality that you must
get everything now."

Who is pushing the three-way stretch? Who is saying that
these are reasonable expectations? The industries that stand
to gain, that's who.

But you don't have to go that route. There are other options. And that's what this book is about.

2. THE FIRST SET OF OPTIONS

Where

If the decision to marry or not to marry has taken an affirmative turn, the choice of where and when to hold the wedding cannot be far behind. Where and when play a major part in setting the tone and personality of your own wedding celebration.

Churches

In the United States a church or house of religious worship has become the site for the majority of wedding ceremonies. This custom is founded in the church as meeting place and social hall as well as in the religious sanctioning of weddings. Historically, there was a time in the early Christian church when it was illegal, or at least frowned upon, to conduct a secular service like a wedding inside the church sanctuary. In the United States today at least one denomination (the Christian Scientists) is not allowed to be married in their church buildings.

However, since the majority of officiants are clergymen and since some religions do not recognize any wedding performed outside their auspices, the custom of the church wedding seems entrenched.

In itself the church wedding can work well for a couple who wants to involve certain elements of tradition and solidarity in their wedding. A church wedding makes at least part of the wedding celebration a wedding service. It is an opportunity for religious blessing and thought, a showcase for the stately ecclesiastical music used at weddings, a recognition of the sense of form, procession, and mystique. To some couples, a wedding in a church is the best statement possible for their public declaration of love. Besides, with the widening tolerance within religious institutions, there is room for innovation in the church ceremony. Most clergy are happy to see a couple who care enough to individualize their wedding service.

On the other hand, the atmosphere of a church automatically fosters roles in a wedding ceremony. It is easier to have guests as spectators in a church, harder to have them become participants. You often find yourself working at your own peril to combat the formality a church imposes. If you take too much liberty, the ceremony seems out of place, trite, or ridiculous. You really can't pretend to be too relaxed and casual.

A church can be an inexpensive place to hold a wedding. If you are not a member of the congregation, you may have to pay $25 to $90 for use of the main worship area (unless you're renting St. Patrick's Cathedral—that's $150). This fee is usually in addition to the gratuity to the clergy or the organist's fee or the fee for use of a reception room within the church. If you just don't have the money, some churches will waive all fees. If you or your parents are members of the congregation, it's all gratis.

If like many couples you are no longer affiliated with a particular church, you are free to choose a church on the basis of location and aesthetic appeal. You might as well choose a particular church for its atmosphere if all other considerations are equal to you. A minister of a handsome Gothic chapel felt that his wedding schedule would be cut in half if his church were less appealing.

You could look for a church that is situated in an area which you find attractive—an old country church, or a church in a seaside setting.

You may not be allowed to use the first church you find. Some congregations put their place of worship off-limits to "outsiders" while others will allow use of their sanctuary for a fee.

Aside from churches, there are many other indoor places to hold a wedding ceremony.

Private Homes

One of your friends or relatives may have the perfect setting for a small, intimate wedding. A house, apartment, yard, garden, courtyard, or patio that particularly pleases you is a fine place to have a wedding with a moderately small number of friends and family. Most of your home-owning friends or relatives would be flattered at a request to house your wedding.

Sometimes the officiant will hold the wedding in his house. This works best if you know the officiant and it isn't a kind of local "wedding palace." For example, a couple was recently married at the home of a judge who was a friend of the groom's father and who was known by the couple. The service included readings from the Jewish prayer book by the groom's mother and the bride's father, along with readings by the bride and groom. There were about thirty-five guests present who grouped around the bride and groom during the ceremony. According to one guest, it was a touchingly intimate occasion and everyone ended up laughing and crying.

Clubs or Organizations with Social Halls

Fraternities, theater guilds, art alliances, ethnic organizations, philosophical and ethical societies, and other groups with large and often beautiful facilities are places to consider for wedding sites. You can choose the one you find most aesthetically pleasing and/or one with which you have a connecting link. Don't give up if you're not a member or if you don't have an "in." Make an appointment to talk to whoever is in charge, show up in person, and see what you can arrange. Moneywise, it usually costs more to rent one of these gathering places, but there are so many variables that no kind of rule on expense could apply to all possibilities. The Grange, VFW, and fire hall fall into this group as do campus buildings.

Art Museums, Opera Houses, Concert Halls, Court Houses, and Other Public Edifices

A public building may hold a certain charm, a personal meaning, or a specific area that would lend itself to your wedding. As long as the site is more pleasing than institutional, it will do nicely.

Art museums, if it can be arranged, are fine places to hold weddings. They often have a courtyard or a specific gallery that the museum asks couples to use. Large buildings with piazzas that are landscaped have become popular wedding sites. One New York City building with a magnificent piazza and fountain (they asked to remain anonymous) will not grant couples permission to marry by the fountain, but they will not stop a wedding.

Arranging for use of such places is somewhat difficult because you have to work around the building's public functions. A careful plan is called for if guests are involved or an uneasy confusion may result.

Hotels

There are pros and cons on hotel weddings. Here's a clergyman's view:

"The worst place to have a wedding is in a hotel. I just hate it. I'll go to all lengths to avoid it and if I can't I charge double. A hotel is by nature a transient place. A rite of some permanency sets up an automatic conflict. As likely as not there is a thin partition separating the wedding from a bowling party on the other side and there are maids accidentally popping in and out. It's the worst of all."

On the pro side, a hotel wedding can be distinguished, it can be quiet or elaborate and arrangements for guests are handled easily.

Finally, two more big considerations. 1) Hotel weddings tend to get flashy and informality is rare. It's often a hyper-staged occasion. 2) Costs are WILD.

Assorted

Art galleries are becoming "in" wedding sites. So are some old historically certified mansions and their attached grounds.

Outdoor Weddings

Outdoor weddings came into vogue during the sixties along with the fleeting flower children. Unlike the flower children, outdoor weddings have stuck. Couples have found that an outdoor setting allows for more casual interpretation of the ceremony, easier choreography, more of a fun atmosphere. The bride and the groom can rid themselves of the mandated traditional formalware and can serve foods and play music more conducive to a celebration where everyone participates.

There are philosophical reasons for weddings held outdoors. Being married outside in a natural setting is reflective of the earth's importance and beauty—it bespeaks a connection to the earth that many young couples are trying to re-establish. Politically, outside weddings are also significant of being married outside the usual institutions of society.

With the wide outdoors to choose from, choices of sites are manifold. Here are some examples:

A summer wedding on the beach at Lake Michigan at around four in the afternoon, was followed, beachside, by a steak grill and drinks from a huge tub of ice studded with bottles of imported beer.

An otherwise traditional wedding was held in American Revolutionary dress on the grounds of Fort Ticonderoga, New York. Bagpipers supplied the music.

A very young couple was married in a ceremony on a Pacific meadow, three miles up the side of a mountain in Oregon. A gentle spray of rain was falling.

The Nantucket Bird Sanctuary was the locale where an art teacher married one of her students.

A ceremony was held in a monastery high up in the mountains of California. One of the brothers officiated. There was wine and fruit afterward.

A cross made of driftwood, erected on a point overlooking the Pacific at Big Sur, was the site for a wedding. There was also a maypole that guests danced around, tying up the bride and groom in its ribbons.

In New York State's Adirondack Preserve, a couple paddled their canoe across Lake Silver to the dock of the summer home of the bride's family. As the couple came into view, a bell began to toll. They were met at the dock by the wedding party and guests who led them in procession to the wedding site.

Curtis Arboretum in Cheltenham Township, Pennsylvania, has been the site of many outdoor weddings among the lovely, huge specimen trees on the grounds.

Beach weddings—up and down both coasts. A wedding to the tune of the surf has grandeur. The horizons opened up by any large body of water will do just as well. On the dock of a Greenwich home on Long Island Sound, a couple was married as the sun rose. Afterward everyone had breakfast on the dock. (NOTE: Weddings on public beaches are best held in the fall—September or October. The crowds are gone; warmth and beauty remain.)

Parks: Local and State, and, If You Can Manage It, National

The National Parks System has no set policy on weddings. To inquire about holding a wedding at a National Park, Recreation Area, Monument, or Historical Site, call the individual director of that site. Because these areas are choked with tourists in the summer, you will probably get a more favorable response if you inquire about an outdoors, off-season wedding with a relatively small number of guests (less than fifty). There are so many beautiful possibilities here. Imagine a wedding near Bridalveil Fall in Yosemite National Park or a beach ceremony on the magnificent coast of Cape Hatteras National Seashore. The parklands in and around Washington, D.C., are used frequently for weddings.

For a list of the preserved lands within the National Park System, look up National Parks in the World Book Encyclopedia. For state and local listings, look to city hall or the county librarian.

State and local parks require the same kind of advance permission with the same kind of variation in response. Some park directors are thrilled at the idea and will give all the help they can. Others are less than enthusiastic, if not prohibitive. There may be costs involved in the form of a permit. These should be minimal, $15 at the most.

Public and Private Gardens, Lawn Areas and Outdoor Campus Areas

If you know someone with a large, lovely garden, courtyard, or an expanse of rolling lawn, ask them about the possibilities of holding a garden wedding (something less elaborate than the White House Rose Garden affair). There are public gardens, specimen gardens, arboretums, and sites of botanical beauty. The good old college green might be perfect. Something about flowers, trees, and other greenery lend a fresh, natural romanticism to a wedding ceremony.

Ranches and Farms

The best thing about ranches and farms is that they usually have a sunny meadow, a pasture, a glade by a river, or some other private place of beauty. Two law students were married on a North Carolina farm belonging to the groom's grandfather. They held the ceremony by a woodland pond on the property and afterward churned buckets of homemade ice cream under a huge tree by the front porch.

City Squares, Courtyards, Malls, Pocket Parks, and Some Playgrounds

The Central Park weddings and Golden Gate Bridge Park weddings are now famous. Smaller and less congested areas of the city are often less subject to interference and are more conducive to a personal celebration. Consider an out-of-the-way time when such an urban area would be used the least. You may need a permit to gather in some cities.

When

The wedding is no longer locked into a Saturday-afternoon time slot. If you have out-of-town guests, most will be able to come only on weekends. Don't rule out Friday night or Sunday. If most of your guests are from the area, you could have the wedding on a weekday evening.

Nothing is fixed. Evening weddings have a whole set of possibilities different from dawn weddings. Both are as "right" as a wedding at high noon. In fact, in very hot weather, or in a situation where there are problems using or obtaining the facilities, early morning and/or evening weddings are probably a boon. Choose a time in accordance to your own preferences and the situations that those preferences will entail.

For example, two architects were married at the architectural focal point of a hundred-year-old church designed by a famous architect whose work they admired. (The focal point happened to be in the center of one of the aisles.) The church was in the heart of the major metropolis where they lived. Both were lovers of the city and knew that early morning is the most delectable moment in the daily cycle of urban activity. They set the ceremony for dawn—5 A.M. The clergyman and both families objected so mournfully that the couple moved the time up to 6 A.M. Thirty people attended despite the early hour. Following the ceremony, everyone went out for a true wedding breakfast at a local restaurant.

Guests

"We didn't want a civil ceremony and we couldn't see a wedding with a cast of thousands. What we wanted was a day to celebrate and share with our friends."

BRUCE and DONNA STERMAN

Another early act of wedding planning is figuring out how many guests are to be invited and who will be members of the wedding party.

Guests are sometimes a trickier matter than one would expect. Determining how many and who has resulted in more than one prewedding dispute. For example, the number of guests can determine the site of the wedding or the site of the wedding can determine the number of guests. The same goes for reception costs. If food is to be served at the reception, it will probably be calculated on a per-head basis by a

caterer or restaurant. Should you set a certain per-head cost
and invite as many guests as you can fit into the amount you
have to spend? Or should you invite everyone you want to
invite and calculate per-head costs on the total number of
people and the amount you have to spend? Is there going to
be a difference between the number of guests who come to
the wedding and the number who are invited to the reception?

It's confusing unless you keep the main objectives in mind.
1) The wedding is your personalized celebration. 2) You'd
like the people who matter most to you to be there. 3) Everyone who comes is coming to celebrate the day with you. If
you buy those objectives, then you'll probably find yourself
choosing the site you want first, asking as many or as few
people as you choose (limited by the site and not by the
costs), and inviting everyone who comes to the wedding to
celebrate with you during and after the ceremony. Costs can
be adjusted around these more important considerations.

When you're figuring the number of guests, establish a
policy that everyone who comes to the wedding comes to the
reception or party afterward. It seems to me obvious and rude
to exclude someone from the celebration after the ceremony
because of financial considerations. If you don't want them
included in the party or if you can't afford their presence,
why invite them in the first place?

The site of the wedding expands or limits the number
of guests. Hometown weddings tend to be larger affairs.
("Oh, we'd better invite the Gleasons from across the street.
They watched you grow up. They'll be hurt if they're not
included.") A wedding in a chapel or private home would
necessarily limit the number of people present.

For some reason, the more people you invite, the more
closely you are tied to a traditional ceremony. Large crowds
of people are hard to manipulate in ways that you may not
have considered. With more people come more expectations,

more pressure, more moves to choreograph. This is less true of outdoor weddings than indoor weddings, but it holds true outdoors, too.

Of course, there are reasons for having a large wedding. Personal reasons. One or both of you may have a close-knit family complete with aunts, uncles, cousins, etc., who you would find it unthinkable to omit. A rabbi says that the most rewarding part of the wedding for him is the grouping to-gether of families—seeing backgrounds and long lines of love spread in the pews behind the young couple. There may be old friends that you want there, past and present fellow employees, the people in the downstairs apartment, and the butcher who cuts you extra slices of meat every now and again. If your love seems to include the majority of everyone you know, then invite them as the wedding site allows.

Some couples find themselves in a situation where their parents are paying off social dues with their wedding. The re-sult is a wedding that must be an *occasion de luxe* to enter-tain friends and business associates who the couple hardly knows. This is the most trying and debasing way to fatten a guest list and in the end almost always means friction and regrets.

There are those wedding manuals that suggest you rule out children under twelve. If you are familiar with the children of friends and family members, it would add to their experience and enrich your celebration to include them. If the reception has such a high per-head cost that it's economi-cally unfeasible to include children, then you might want to reconsider the purposes behind the reception.

Children start somewhere around the age of three. Younger than that they're babies who are wont to cry and are sure to limit their parents' social maneuvers. But then, that's stereo-typing babies. In Boston, three bridesmaids marched in procession in a garden wedding, each carrying a bouquet of flowers. The fourth and last marched in the processional carrying a five-month-old baby—her own. She thought he was the best adornment she could bring to the occasion. The bride, a close friend, agreed. The child lay quiet and happy throughout the ceremony.

Attendants

Bridesmaids and groomsmen probably originated from the practice of bridal capture. Sometimes this was a real kidnaping of a woman and sometimes it was a kind of game with all the major participants back in time for the wedding. The bridesmaids attended to the bride's clothing and protected her while the groomsmen watched for any would-be captors. The attendants at the wedding also served as witnesses to the ceremony.

Although no one has stolen an American bride for years (it was a sporting activity in Pioneer days), the attendants are still a big part of the wedding. They have come to represent friendship and close ties and support at the wedding ceremony.

There is nothing mandatory about having wedding attendants. If you'd prefer to go without a retinue, then you are free to do so. If you are having a tiny wedding, all you will need in most states is two witnesses and they needn't serve any role other than that. Large weddings (e.g., Princess Anne Elizabeth Alice Louise of Great Britain) needn't have attendants either. In fact if you want your wedding to be rather singular, then you might be better off omitting the wedding party. By doing so, you'd omit the indecision of who to ask, what they should wear, rehearsal for every one, and so on. (Let's not even talk about establishment tedium like "The Bridesmaids Luncheon.")

Many couples do want their friends to participate with them in the marriage ceremony. It seems a warm and appropriate way to share the close ties of the day.

How many attendants should you have? If you are having a relatively small wedding, you might not want to make it "top heavy" with scores of attendants. If you are having a wedding within a church, where the ushers are seating people, the number of attendants could be based on a reasonable estimate of the number of guests that will need to be ushered down the aisle. (If you do want your guests to wait and be seated by ushers, have enough ushers to avoid a pile up in the back of the church.)

The whole concept of ushering people to their seats is a very formal, stilted gesture. You may, or may not, want to eliminate this custom as being too pompous for the type of wedding you're planning. You could change the role of ushers and bridesmaids to one of being greeters who stand at the door where guests enter, hand out programs, take coats, give each guest a flower, and/or point out the area where the guests can help themselves to a seat, with no stuffiness like the bride's side and groom's side.

For some reason it has become the custom to have the same number of bridesmaids and ushers. This may form a neat symmetry at the altar, but it's not necessary. It probably started as an outgrowth of the faulty choreography used in many recessionals where the bridesmaids and ushers team up in pairs to leave the church. (See chapter 7.) If you have one best man and four bridesmaids, that's fine. The reverse is fine too. This allows for more freedom in choosing the people you really want to be attendants. There are no "slots" in the wedding party to be filled.

Recently there has been a trend toward having a large group of friends serve as attendants. A kind of "best people" movement. Sixteen such friends surrounded a couple as they were married on a cliff overlooking Frenchman's Bay in Maine. The wedding in the Adirondack Preserve mentioned earlier included a number of friends and family members who served as "best people." Group support like this is in keeping with the communal spirit of many weddings.

In asking people to be members of your wedding, consider only your feelings about having them close to you during your ceremony and helping you to prepare for the ceremony. Ask friends you love . . . regardless of their looks, weight, height, or month of pregnancy.

One of the functions of the wedding party is to aid in preparation for the wedding. Don't feel that this is imposing on anyone. When you ask each attendant to be in the wedding, include some idea of how you want him or her to help you out. Most friends will be anxious to give a hand in the plans and may come up with terrific suggestions and methods of operation. If you delegate responsibilities to those you trust, you can avoid the insane amount of detail work that seems to crop up with every wedding—even small, simple ceremonies. Besides, preparations worked out as a group are usually fun and can represent an act of love in themselves.

Do you want a flower girl and a ring bearer? Consider their origins. They are outright fertility symbols representing children to come from the union. If that speaks your own view of the marriage, then they would seem to fit. Many couples today are doing without children as wedding attendants for symbolic reasons. They don't think of their marriage in terms of fertility and child-bearing any more.

There are practical reasons, too. A petrified little flower girl is capable of just about anything. Ring bearers have been known to wet their velvet pants at crucial moments. And, of course, there is the frightening hassle of which little cousin, neighbor, or friend's child is to be chosen in the first place. Older children can serve as wedding attendants with a good deal of pride and understanding. They are not "baby" symbols and are not asked for their cuteness quotient. They play a real part whereas younger kids are often for show.

Wedding Rehearsal

Ideally, everyone should be relaxed enough to have the kind of wedding where nothing can go wrong and, if it does, incorporate it into the wedding proceedings. In such happy instances a wedding rehearsal would be unthinkable.

While some weddings need no rehearsal, those weddings that do can be overrehearsed. Especially the "cast of thousands" kind. ("Everyone on stage for the Hawaiian scene.") If the members of the wedding party are concentrating so heavily on where they should stand and at what point in the ceremony they should move, they become self-aware and never get into the proceedings at all.

Small weddings held in a chapel, private home, garden, hillside, etc., don't need a rehearsal. Large church weddings with more than seventy-five guests probably call for a rehearsal—a brief and casual one.

At the rehearsal, music is co-ordinated and choreography is smoothed out. The ceremony is not read at the rehearsal. The ceremony is a one-time piece of business and does not get rehearsed. That's part of the special high experience of your own wedding day.

An officiant may or may not charge for the rehearsal time. Ditto for a musician or church music director. (If there is any traveling done by the officiant to attend the rehearsal, he will probably charge a small fee.)

You may want to get together after the rehearsal for a party or a bite to eat. The expensive formality of a proper rehearsal dinner is truly unnecessary. Since the rehearsal has grouped together people who are friends anyway, there should be no bother deciding where to get together and what to do for a good time.

Published Announcements

There is really no reason to announce the marriage or engagement of two people and then show a picture of just one. Why not have a picture taken of the two of you? A portrait head shot of you both would be fine for an engagement announcement. Better yet, why not a more natural shot in the park, or at a table? Anything flattering, not too posed, and non-suggestive is reasonable. For a wedding announcement, a shot of the couple after the wedding, looking somewhat pleased, is more descriptive than a formal bridal portrait.

For some reason, wedding photos of couples are common practice in many small communities and in the West. I don't know why the young women of these communities have leapt from their pedestals in this matter while their more established (and supposedly more aware) eastern sisters are still showing angelic bridal portraits.

Some newspapers do have restrictions enforcing "female only" photos in their wedding and engagement blurbs. It seems that these photo restrictions hold tighter for engagement announcements than for wedding announcements. If you feel strongly about a "female only" display photo, don't send a photo at all.

If the photographs in wedding announcements tell a distorted story, the copy that follows is twice as distorting. It is an unabashed status report. Prime example: the Society Page of the New York Sunday *Times*. The young couple is known only by the college or school they attended, the names of their grandparents, and the place of business of their father. Any other notes of prestige are included. Not only is it elitist, it's rather sad.

Most newspapers are inflexible about the copy that follows the photos. You are often sent a form to fill out with the usual categories of lineage. Fill out only what you want the newspaper to print. If your wedding has been innovative or non-traditional, write the details on the back of the form. If it's newsworthy enough, the paper might print it in lieu of the status rundown.

Engagement announcements are more difficult. Try to include real and important facts about your lives. If it falls too short of form, the paper may choose not to print it.

There is no law that says the announcement must be placed in the Sunday paper. The Sunday society pages are crowded because most people suppose that the notice will get more attention if it is published on a day when people customarily read the paper. Why not Tuesday? Wednesday? Friday? You can avoid the Sunday "Weddings of the Week" line-up. If you have details other than the usual format that you want included, you have a better chance on a day other than Sunday. However, don't pick Saturday. Nobody reads a paper on Saturday—and every advertiser knows it. Saturday is thin paper day.

Be aware that putting your name in the paper subjects you to all the commercial interests who can figure out your address. Given that your parents' names—first, last, and middle —are included in the announcement, the chances of finding out how to reach you are very good. At-home addresses in the paper make you prey to all sorts of mail, door-to-door types, and even robbers.

A couple who was married in 1972 got fifty-six pieces of unsolicited mail as a direct result of their address appearing in a daily newspaper listing of marriage licenses granted at City Hall. After their wedding, they got four telephone calls from life insurance salesmen and were broken into and robbed of the wedding presents which were still piled on the floor. The only extreme element in this incident is the robbery. The mail and the salesmen get everybody.

Theoretically, a newspaper should be a vehicle to announce

the important points of an event—your wedding. When important gets translated to status, it becomes debatable whether you should allow a public communication to misrepresent you. Some papers are more lenient than others, some are anxious for a "new wedding" story to freshen up their retitled women's pages.

Use the facilities of a newspaper announcement only if it will announce the wedding that really occurred.

3. PREWEDDING PSYCH-OUTS

"The three months before our wedding were just hell. We almost didn't get married. Charles walked out two times and I was upset all the time. Looking back, it's hard to say exactly what it was that upset us so much. The plans and the money and everything had an awful lot to do with it, I guess."

Couple married in 1974

There are many decisions and relationships that come into play during the period before a wedding. It can be a terribly confusing and frustrating time. The establishment-wedding rules take it for granted that you're going to run yourself ragged over the wedding preparations. And it's not always easier if you're discarding the rules and branching out on your own. The following are three areas of stress that must be dealt with and that often erupt in contention: the groom's involvement, wedding financing, and family pressure.

The Forgotten Groom and the Frantic Bride

The women's movement has been promising for some time that its efforts for personal equality will eventually liberate the American male. No one needs more liberation than the American male who is about to serve some time playing the role of Groom. The establishment-wedding psychology all too frequently turns the Groom into a token symbol at his own wedding and makes the Bride an overblown, well-financed parody of the event.

Almost everybody does it. Think wedding and you think

bride. Traditionally, brides and their mothers end up swirling around in a buzz of plans and missions and the groom often gets left out in the cold. Occasionally he'll be consulted or told what is happening. But for the most part, he is expected to pay for what he is supposed to pay for and show up at the church on time.

Lots of grooms get the wedding-bell jitters in traditional situations because communications are at an all-time low. The bride sometimes doesn't see her intended because she has too much to do. When she does see him, the talk is all wedding. As the day of the wedding nears, the duress reaches such a peak that the groom begins to suspect that the wedding itself is the *raison d'être* of the relationship. He feels as if he got the whole show on the road with his proposal and now the monstrous production is being carried out with only a token role for him.

Meanwhile the bride in this situation is growing busier and more frantic. She is being treated with deference by family members and particularly by commercial interests. ("And which type of stationery would our BRIDE prefer?") Her stardom is continually reinforced.

Some brides get so bowled over at the thought of their only wedding day, the one and only day when they must look radiant and be blissfully charming, that they freeze. Nothing is good enough, nothing is quite as perfect as it should be. Their decision-making powers start to disintegrate. How can they be sure when there is so much at stake?

But a bride alone does not represent the wedding. Her beauty or the whiteness of her gown or her flowers are not where it's at. A couple represents the wedding. And the venture of together planning and carrying out a personalized celebration is an exciting, special action that should end up bringing a man and woman in love closer together. Fortunately, this is happening more and more. Couples live together before marriage and/or live in an away-from-home area that puts them out of reach of parental pressure. They plan the wedding together, execute the plans, and get married as a pair of individuals. And that's how it should be.

Money—Realistic Approaches to Realistic Problems

Whoever it was that first uttered the adage "he who pays the piper calls the tune," was no doubt in a situation where the tune was "Here Comes the Bride." The financing of weddings can involve major transactions and major headaches. This book, hopefully, points out ways you can save or eliminate wedding costs. But there is no such thing as a free wedding. Even city hall ceremonies cost something. Somebody has to pay and that somebody usually wants a say in decisions involving the wedding plans.

Bridal-etiquette books go into great lengths over "Who Pays for What." The rules are firm—the bride or her family pays for the ceremony, the groom or his kin puts up the honeymoon. All minor expenditures are covered—from the white aisle carpet runner (bride) to the boutonnieres (groom). Sometimes the groom's family offers to chip in for the reception and the bride's family may accept the offer if they must, or wish to.

These rules make the traditional wedding an orderly rite with established precedents. Both families can avoid the delicately trying subject of money during this tentative period of their relationship. It is not a democratic system. The bride's family bears the great burden of the cost. But all this goes along with the understanding of the traditional wedding.

That understanding expands into all the other areas of established bridal procedure. If the families of the bride and groom are asked to follow a traditional "Who-Pays-for-What" schedule, they might well expect a wedding that follows most of the other establishment standards. And who would question their reasoning?

If your wedding is to be largely traditional, then the etiquette-approved payment schedule may avoid confusion, as it was designed to do. If your wedding is to be highly individualized, then the payment schedule will be meaningless. (Who pays for the balloons and incense?)

Traditional or non-traditional, there is still the question of who influences decisions about how money is to be spent. Planning and financing a wedding is a particularly difficult problem for young people who are no longer living with their parents. Many young people leave for their four years of college and never really come home again. They become used to planning their own lives and deciding their own likes and dislikes long before they choose to marry. Others make the break not through college but by growing away into apartments and lives of their own. Then all of a sudden it's time for their parents to step in and give them a wedding. The old rules of etiquette make possible some of the catastrophes that occur during this period when the bride is artificially thrust back under the wings of her family in preparation for her being correctly delivered to the safety of her new husband's name. Parents and children alike find it damned hard to handle.

For the answer to all this, you'll have to size up your relationship with the purse holder in your life. If you have a harmonious relationship with your purse holder and if you can concur on most plans for the wedding, then you're home free. If you anticipate trouble with moneyed interests muscling in on the wedding plans, then you'll need to find an approach to satisfy all parties.

Here now is a brief and stereotyped example:

A: Harold and I have a great idea—an organic beans and franks barbecue for the reception!

B: Dear, I was thinking more in terms of tea sandwiches, petit fours, maybe crackers and caviar. . . .

A: Come on, I hate all that nibbling ladies' food. Let's have an honest-to-God meal or something.

B: Now you realize that with a semiformal afternoon wedding a meal isn't really . . . uh, proper. What's called for is light refreshment, maybe buffet style at most.

Now here the conversation could take on an important turn. It could go:

A: So how about beans and franks buffet style?

B: Well I suppose we could have that along with some chicken salad to make a light buffet meal.

A: Sure. And Sue could bake some of her whole wheat raisin bread.

B: I guess that would be alright.

And so on. Negotiations will proceed. However, the conversation could have gone on like this:

A: Nothing doing. I insist that we have something more solid than tea sandwiches. Proper—who cares?

B: Listen here. I'm paying for this and all my friends will be there and we're going to give a decent reception.

A: Who's wedding is this anyway? Harold and I and all *our* known friends love beans and franks. . . .

This conversation is entrenching for a full-scale battle. Eventually more voices than A and B will be involved and there will be sides taken and bad feelings and an over-all escalation of tension.

Dealing only in reality, consider your own situation. Who controls the purse strings? One person? A pair of people? More than a pair of people? (The more people involved in decisions about how money is to be spent, the more complicated the decisions will be.) What are the purse holder's stakes in the wedding? What does this person want for himself? What does he or she want for you?

Would a conversation with your purse holder fall closer to the first ending or the second ending? Can you disagree without either of you coming apart? Can you compromise comfortably with him or her? Does this person see some validity in the way you live your life and can you understand his or her viewpoints on life?

The words purse holder and the neutral tag of "person" have been used here in order to give some relief from the emotionalized reality that most purse holders are parents. They command a great sway on your decision-making powers. They have no doubt influenced your decision to marry the person you've chosen, if not by present influence then by the consistent environmental influence that goes back to the day of your birth. It could be argued that you're marrying your intended because of them or despite them.

But then it comes to wedding plans and there needs to be a better approach than "because of or despite of."

If you have every reason to believe that you and your purse holder can compromise and concur through the forests of wedding detail, then proceed within the context of purse holder and recipient. You can use the "Who Pays for What" rules or you could choose to disregard the rules entirely. However, if you're not looking forward to planning with the moneyed interests or if you'd just like to take the responsibility on yourself, there are alternative courses open to you.

1. Finance Your Own Wedding

Use your own money because of independence; use it because of generosity; use it because you've got it. Never use it out of spite. Your whole purpose is soiled before starting if you march in with an attitude that says, "Get lost I'm doing this my way with my money and that means you stay out of it." Your purse holders are just as excited about the wedding as the two of you are. They can accept your desire for financial independence if it's not accompanied with rejection motives.

If your purse holders are disappointed about not being able to give you a big splurge for your wedding, they might feel that they've done something for you by giving the two of you an important wedding present: a contribution toward a new car, a plot of land, or some other major gift that will be long used and long remembered. If you're planning to take a honeymoon trip after the wedding, you might offer to take care of the ceremony and reception if your purse holders will pay for the trip.

Financing your own wedding is sometimes not a matter of choice. Many prospective brides and grooms do not have a purse holder in their lives. If this is the case, then family related problems may center around the sensitivity of parents unable or unwilling to put up money for their children's wedding. The unwilling ones usually come around. Fathers who have opposed matches on their sacred honors have been known to wear the widest smile in the house on the day of the wedding. The parents who are unable to afford a wedding need to be dealt with gently. They'll need to feel proud of you and proud of themselves on your wedding day. Make them know that they've given you a lot already.

When the two of you do decide to pay for your own wedding, pool your resources and put the money for wedding expenses into a separate bank account. Having all cash for the wedding set apart helps keep spending within the realities of the account's balance. It also eliminates the confusion of "Shall I pay for this or will you?" And best of all, it makes it all more exciting—a joint venture.

Don't get nervous if you find yourselves low on cash. With some originality and ingenuity money is no problem. Really! The two of you can make the plans and take the responsibility on yourselves for their execution or you could ask friends and relatives for special favors. Almost everyone is happy to help a bride and groom. Think of ways to wipe out expensive aspects of the wedding and ways to add emphasis to less expensive elements. Haggle with suppliers. Borrow anything but money. Make and even make do. The scope of your resourcefulness will determine the cost.

One great wedding on the beach with twenty-five guests and a delicious wedding breakfast cost the bride and groom a total of $80, counting their clothes, invitations, license, minister—everything except the rings. The food was provided and cooked by friends and the breakfast itself was held at the beach house of the groom's aunt. There are variations on this fine little wedding with equally non-hyped costs.

If you're doing it on your own, do it with what you have, along with a little non-financial help from your friends. Usually everyone ends up feeling really good about the whole thing.

2. Spending Their Money Your Way

Sometimes purse holders can be very reasonable about turning the money and the planning over to you. Perhaps they're not really looking forward to all the wedding getting and spending and they would be content to let you handle it. You might have a meeting with your purse holders, tell them your plans, and, if they agree in general, ask them to put the amount they intended to spend in a bank account so you can make the plans and pay the bills. Sneak in a word or two on your own behalf, citing your demonstrated ability to handle your own finances. Assure them that any leftover money will be put toward your first home (car, education, trip to Greece, etc.). This sounds too unbelievably simple to even suggest. It's an obvious solution, beneficial to both parties if everyone trusts everyone else. Air it for discussion.

Or, you could bargain for the right to spend the money your way. Ask the purse holders how much they intended to spend on the wedding. Offer to give yourselves a "recogniz-able" wedding for one half, two thirds, or three quarters that amount. Offer your plans and consider their suggestions. When you've agreed on major issues such as the size and tone of the wedding, where it will be held and what, if any, celebration will follow, agree on a sum allotted to you. Ask if you may keep any money left over from this amount. When all this is decided, you may find yourselves with the options that go with spending the money as you see fit as well as the possibility of leftover money to motivate ingenious spending.

Once the money is given to you to spend, there should be no breach on either side as far as major understandings go. You would not suddenly decide to change the wedding loca-tion from a church to a clover field nor would the purse holders start badgering for little matters that had been turned over to your discretion along with the money agree-ment.

3. *Give the Reception to Your Purse Holders*

If your purse holders must finance the wedding and if plans and compromises are not going well, perhaps the only alter-native is to divide up the whole wedding into separate areas of decision. Ask the purse holders to decide and finance the reception. You decide and finance the wedding ceremony. Perhaps it would work better for you the other way around. You must judge for yourself what is most important to the two of you—the wedding ceremony or the party that fol-lows. Most couples feel that the wedding service must be authentically theirs.

This is a big compromise. After a marvelously individual-ized wedding, a couple piles into a car heading for Dad's Country Club or, for that matter, Dad's Grange Hall, to celebrate the way Dad and Mom and all their friends and relatives like to do it. It's a compromise that makes it worth-

while to consider giving yourself a tiny jewel of a wedding
with close family and friends and trimmings to match your
own bank account. But if it is the only way to keep all of you
from going mad, then it must be considered as a compromise
solution. As some divorce lawyers recognize a good settle-
ment by one that satisfies neither party, then this situation,
completely satisfying to neither party, might be the answer.
(How did the divorce lawyers get in here?)

Don't ask. But while we're on the gloomy subject, there's
another point to consider. As crass as it seems, parents who
invest a great deal of money in their children's wedding have
a large financial stake in the marriage working out. A gigantic
wedding puts a burden on two people who are trying to unite
their lives. All that hoopla, all those presents. They'll be disappointing everyone if they don't make a go of it. If after
a short time it appears that the marriage isn't going to work,
the couple may have guilt feelings as grandiose as the
wedding.

Family Pressures

Weddings used to be tribal occasions, community occasions. Family and friends would gather together, representing
an important social function. Of course, many weddings still
are. But in just as many instances today, the community is
no longer there. If the bride and groom did grow up with a
home town, they feel no compunction to return to it for
marriage unless it is convenient, or they are pressured to do
so. It seems more realistic to them to be married in venue
because of the life that they have established as their own,
the friends that are part of that life, and the desirability of
the chosen location.

Besides, the old community cannot really be reconstructed.
Too much has changed. Our tribal units are thinning out and
can no longer be supported by the representation of family

and a few friends. Our adopted communities allow us far more freedom than our tribal units did. And they offer freedom because they offer less possessiveness as well as less of the caring that goes with a close-knit, possessive unit. Be that as it may.

A couple today may or may not run into this disparity of view about the functions of a wedding. If an extended family is somewhere in the background, they probably will. You will have to explain why the First Methodist Church of South Elmsville is not a reasonable place for you to hold your wedding ceremony. Why a kosher reception is not a factor to be considered. Why Father O'Conner will not be asked to perform the ceremony. And somewhere along this line of thought you will have to formulate a strong philosophy as to whether the wedding is for you and your own life styles or for your family and a life style that is an important part of your past.

For couples who want a wedding more in tune with the way they live their lives, there may be tricky moments. Of course you will want family and old friends present. How do you hold the wedding you want without alienating the old guard and stirring up a storm on the eve of a joyous celebration? Even holding the purse strings you may find that there are certain family expectations you don't intend to meet that will have to be broached gently.

One of the best ways to hold the family at bay is to give them all something to do. If you step in and ask specific favors of family members or old friends, they will feel themselves part of the celebration and will be much less apt to criticize your plans. One bride asked the groom's mother to silk-screen the cover of a wedding program. The mother was a fair-to-good artist and took such care and time in making the programs that she was barely heard from. She felt great about the comments that were made about the program—it turned out quite well—and she had nothing but enthusiastic things to say about her son's wedding. This same mother had been deeply critical of the early wedding plans.

Family and friends can be called upon to participate in many of the preparations: reading special selections, poems, or prayers at the service, helping to sew, prepare food, decorate, lend linens, glasses, or sentimental tokens to be carried on the day of the wedding. It usually works out ideally; you can plan your wedding your way and have your family's generous support at the same time. If you are in easygoing control of the situation, any unfavorable criticisms or outdated expectations gradually fade away.

At one point in the ceremony of a church wedding in 1973, the family was greeted and a kind of leave-taking was symbolized. The two immediate families sat in the first two rows of the church. Before the rings were exchanged, an organ interlude was played while the couple walked over to each family, kissed them, and thanked them for being what they had been all their lives. It was a touching moment—one that meant a lot to two families who didn't wholeheartedly understand the non-traditional wedding that ensued.

Involving family members and older friends doesn't necessarily mean that they are dissidents. A Boston couple asked an older friend to be their "paraclete." He would offer them advice and support throughout their marriage. This couple felt very keenly the breakdown of the emotional support units in society. They included the role of paraclete in the wording of the ceremony. At the ceremony, he pledged to assist them when they had a problem, individually or as a couple.

Again, personal innovation is easier for couples who have been away from home for a time, who have started their own lives, who are not marrying the boy or girl next door. But even parents of a couple who have not yet cut family ties are more inclined to give way to young ideas if these ideas are presented with reasons to back up their meaningfulness and are expressed as a joint desire. A couple presenting plans in a well-stated joint effort usually find themselves greeted with acceptance and respect.

However, sometimes you just can't please everybody. You won't be happy with your wedding if you end up sacrificing your own desires to a "My mother always dreamed this is how it would be" line of thought. If you run into brick-wall opposition, be tactful, be decided, be gentle, and proceed with your plans. Weddings do have a way of changing people. Family members who vow that they will never attend such an affair show up and have a good time. That happens so often. Sooner or later opposition softens in the face of love.

4. YOUR OWN WEDDING RING

The Past

Wedding rings are an ancient tradition. Circular bands made of iron, brass, copper, or gold can be traced back to the Greek and Roman eras. At that time they were regarded as protective good-luck charms as well as symbols of marriage.

Beginning with the Middle Ages the only rings involved in a marriage were presented at a betrothal ceremony. These rings pledged the prospective bride and groom to marry each other in the future. Sometimes a third ring was included, worn by a witness to the betrothal. Such rings grew to be tricky affairs, with matching links or hinges that formed the three rings into one when all were fitted together. The groom, or his representative, slipped the betrothal ring onto the prospective bride's third finger, left hand. It was erroneously thought that a vein or nerve ran directly from that finger to the heart. Favorite designs embossed on the rings were two joined hands, a pair of hearts pierced by an arrow, or a heart held in the palm of a hand. Later, as women acquired more jewelry throughout their lifetimes, the wedding ring became a plain band in order to set it apart from fancier costume rings.

Supposedly, the first diamond wedding ring on record was given to Mary of Burgundy in 1477 by the anxious Emperor of Austria. For some reason he thought Mary would say "no," so he wanted to impress her and the family in a big way. A tradition was born.

But it is a tradition that was less adhered to in the past

than in recent times. All of the precious stones were regarded as usual and appropriate for wedding rings. Plain wedding bands were never forgotten either. Queen Elizabeth, upon her marriage to Philip, refused to have her wedding ring adorned with gems, but "chose to be wedded with a plain hoop of gold like any other maiden."

The Present

If you want wedding rings, you hopefully will want to be wearing them for some time. Since this is an important decision, it's one that the two of you should make together. The scene of the ardent suitor kneeling before his beloved with a prepurchased diamond is present-day material for commercials and cartoonists.

Draw up a joint mental outline of what you are looking for before you set out to go ring shopping. This doesn't mean you can't change your mind later if you see something you prefer more than your original intentions. It does mean that you've thought through the reasons for your initial choice and those reasons will be out in the open to gauge any interesting alternatives that arise. Do decide on price. It is impossible to set an arbitrary figure beforehand. However, you can draw a maximum/minimum range to keep you realistic in the face of the huge prices that slip glibly from the lips of jewelers. Things to consider:

Do you both want rings?

Do you want wedding bands for each of you or an engagement ring plus wedding band for the bride?

Do either of you want gems? There is no reason why the groom can't have a gem set in his ring if he wants one.

If yes to gems, would you prefer a diamond to another stone? Why?

Do you want matching rings or would you each prefer a different style?

Do you like the traditional look, contemporary design, or an antique-style of jewelry?

Is there another piece of jewelry or another symbol you would rather use than the wedding ring?

Will you feel satisfied about investing a large amount of money in a wedding ring? Will you be satisfied with a small investment?

Finding a Jeweler

Many people don't realize that there is a genuine difference between a jeweler's store and a jewelry store.

A jeweler sells gems and settings. He can sell you a gem and then sell you any setting in which he will hand set your stone. Or, he can sell you an already set ring from one of his showcases. Sometimes a jeweler will create a setting for you if you don't like any of those he has in stock or any of the ones he can order. Your choices of gem/setting combinations are myriad. A jeweler buys gems and settings at wholesale prices and sells them at retail prices which depend on his particular overhead and competition.

A jewelry store, or the jewelry department of a large store, sells ready-made stock that has been shipped to them from a supplier. All of their rings probably will come from a commercial, nationally known line of jewelry. They cannot set the stone you want in the setting you want; they can only sell you what they have in stock. Their prices are based on the retail price as authorized by the supplier rather than relying strictly on overhead or competition.

The quality of a ring bought from a nationally known line of jewelry is closely controlled and you can be assured that

you are indeed buying what you're paying for. You are relying on the reputation of a manufacturer of wedding rings
rather than the reputation of an individual jeweler. (Incidentally, the jeweler may also carry the same line of stock in addition to his own rings.)

All this information is more important to couples looking
for gem rings or unusual rings than to those seeking wedding
bands. Commercial wedding bands are much the same everywhere. Jewelers order most of their supply from the same
sources that jewelry stores use. The place with the widest
selection of wedding bands is the place to shop. A chance for
a different or an adapted band, however, will be found only
at the jeweler's.

A reputable jeweler's store is one that has been around
long enough to have pleased a certain number of customers
and to have stayed in business through reputable practice. If
money is an object, then avoid all stores with a high overhead—and this especially means prestige jeweler's stores.
Brahmin-type stores can charge a fat percentage for their
name, even in "lower priced" jewelry. If you feel that you
must buy your ring from the store where the movie stars and
the social register hang out, then be prepared to pay for that
privilege. Make sure you understand why purchasing your
ring from a prestige store makes a difference to you.

Many metropolitan areas have a "jewelers' row" location.
For some reason a number of jewelers seem to set up shop in
one particular street or surrounding blocks. Try these shops
first. Competition will keep prices down, and fellow jewelers
peppered throughout the area usually keep each other honest.

Size up the jeweler's window. If the display window is filled
with incredibly junky jewelry—huge conglomerate lumps of
gold that offend your eye on sight—then don't even walk in.
You're going to need to trust the taste and good judgment of
the jeweler you choose. All jewelers must carry what the trade
demands. There are people who delight in obnoxious jewelry

and for some reason those people buy a lot of it. A merchant must supply them or lose business. Find a store that has a healthy representation of jewelry in the display window that looks well designed to you. Then go in and talk to the jeweler.

Buying a Diamond

If you intend to buy a diamond ring, the most important thing to keep in mind is that you can shop around. Most people would shop very carefully if they were out to purchase a new car or a new stereo. But many people, when faced with a caseful of diamonds and a convincing salesman, feel obligated to buy what they like at the first price they hear. Even jewelers admit that easily half of young couples purchasing diamonds buy a ring from the first store they walk into. Buying a diamond ring is evidently a very intimidating process.

The best reason for shopping around is that you will find the diamond that pleases you most only by looking at a great number of diamonds. You'll be surprised how expert you become after a couple of days of diamond shopping. Diamonds are best compared by putting them side by side on two fingers and sizing them up at close range. You can judge the best shape for your hand, spot any flaws in your stone, and compare sparkle and luster.

Have the diamond salesman show you what he has within your price range. He has plenty of stock and should have plenty of time for prospective customers. Get him to point out flaws. Ask to see the stone under a jeweler's eyepiece. Look for black carbon specks (bad flaws), white specks, and yellowishness. Look for flaws in the cutting—the worst of these are visible, but most are invisible to untrained eyes. Hardly any diamonds are flawless and a large part of the stone's price depends on the existing flaws, or as the jeweler may call it, the clarity.

Another good reason to shop around is price. Jewelers are individuals and for the amount you have to spend you might find the perfect diamond for you at one store that costs less than a comparable diamond at a different store.

A good approach to buying a ring at a jeweler's store is to purchase the stone first and then look for an appealing setting. Usually people tend to think of the ring as a whole and for this reason put too much emphasis on the setting. The gem is the key factor of a diamond ring, or any ring with a precious stone. You might feel that you could get a good buy on a diamond at one store and purchase the setting you like most at another. Feel free to do so.

Options

A number of young couples want a more individual wedding ring than a diamond solitaire or an ordinary gold band. Often members of this group don't know quite what it is they do want, although they know for sure that the traditional approach isn't enough for them. They are hunting out their own traditions.

Manufacturers are tuned in to the urge for originality and the newer styles of commercial wedding bands can sometimes satisfy a craving for the different. New looks of barklike gold, textured gold, etched gold, and the free-form "mottled" gold may be just far enough from the traditional wedding band to please the individualist. The recent introduction of enamel wedding bands has lent a bit of color to a once all-gold piece of jewelry. One recently married couple bought similar, but not identical, wedding bands that were formed from geometrical designs of enamel. His was made of gold squares filled with deep purple enamel. Hers was bright green ovals of enamel. They are a matched set of wedding bands without being "look alikes."

Before the nineteenth century, silver rings were more common than gold ones, though gold was more desired. (Martin Luther wore a silver wedding ring.) However, silver is a very soft metal and not good construction material for a ring that will be constantly worn. In a matter of years, a silver wedding band would be badly scratched and perhaps even bent. White gold is more sturdy if a silver hue rather than a yellow-gold hue is what you have in mind.

The diamond as the only expression of love worthy of a wedding ring is a concept that is up for question. Jewelers persist that four out of five engaged couples want a diamond ring. It is this very percentage that is weighing heavily against the diamond in the minds of couples who are more open to other gem possibilities.

The diamond is considered a precious stone. Also in the precious-stone category are rubies, sapphires, and emeralds. The cost of these precious stones can be more or less than a diamond, depending on size and flaws. The emerald is the most expensive of the three and vies with the diamond for high prices. For the amount you'd plan to pay for a medium-small diamond, you could have a much larger, better quality ruby, or a stunning sapphire. These gems could be set as traditionally or non-traditionally as you prefer.

All the birthstones, other than the precious stones already mentioned, are considered semiprecious. Each of the semiprecious gems has its own particular beauty regardless of its monetary value as a gem. Some, like the turquoise, are considered more semi than precious. However, the price is not the first factor in choosing a stone for your wedding ring. Perhaps the tranquility of a pearl or the glow of a topaz best state your particular preferences for a gem or for each other. Please don't feel that your birthstone has to be your favorite stone. The birthstones have been assigned anonymously to the particular months over which they rule and this designation has little to do with your options unless you want it to. Maybe if you met in the month of March, or decided to marry in

March, the aquamarine, March's stone, might work its way into your choices. You can certainly allow yourselves to indulge in outright sentimentality for a decision about your wedding ring.

All of the following stones are readily available in varying costs and are beautifully suitable for either a "male" or "female" ring:

Garnet	Onyx	Opal
Amethyst	Aquamarine	Tourmaline
Bloodstone	Peridot	Pearl
Moonstone	Topaz	Turquoise

Other attractive stones to consider which are not associated with any particular months are:

Tigereye	Coral	Jade
Lapis	Abalone	

These are by no means complete lists. You might find a lesser known stone that to you far outshines the above offerings.

Semiprecious stones and precious stones can be cut in two general ways: faceted and cabochon. The faceted style is the most familiar precious-gem cut. It consists of cutting faces and angles in the stone to catch light, causing the stone to sparkle. A diamond is always cut with facets and the style of these facets varies with the shape: square cut, marquis, oval, brilliant, or round cut. A cabochon (kà/bŏ/shôn) cut is a stone that has been cut and polished into a smooth, rounded surface. The shape of the stone may be round, oval, or even marquis.

As a rule, opaque stones such as turquoise, opal, and moonstone are cut in cabochon style. Transparent stones like garnets or topaz may be cut in either cabochon or faceted manner. The fewer imperfections in an uncut stone, the higher degree of clarity, the more probability that it will be cut with facets to take advantage of its potential sparkle. It follows then that cabochon stones are less expensive than faceted stones because their potential quality was not as good. This may be true. But it is not to infer that stones cut cabochon style are inferior. They are merely a different look, one you may prefer. Stones cut in cabochon style are particularly suited to contemporary geometrical settings.

Thoughts on simulated stones: They're not the real thing. This is true for the barely simulated, very cheap birthstones and for the more expensive simulated stones such as the mock star sapphires. These mock stones with a starlike gleam and cabochon cut are not even semiprecious. They're made from a chemical process. They're fairly inexpensive and adaptable and come in a wide variety of colors. But they're about as rare and individual as a plastic flower. For the same amount of money you could choose one of the less costly semiprecious gems.

Original Rings

Despite the expanse of choices that can be found at a jeweler's, there is a rising demand for custom-designed wedding rings.

Why?

Because an original ring can be designed to your own specifications or to the limit of the designer's range of talent.

Because it is crafted by hand.

Because it is very personally yours. Nobody in the world has rings like yours but the two of you. They are as unique as your own personalities.

You probably haven't heard very much about personally designed wedding rings. Certainly women's magazines or the bridal magazines don't mention them in deference to their diamond ring advertisers. A jeweler who deals mostly in manufactured settings won't encourage you to look into original jewelry. And your friends may have never run across the idea either. Despite this lack of information, investigating the possibilities of personally designed rings may be worth the effort if you are serious about finding an individualistic piece of wedding jewelry. The cost can be high or reasonable and the results are usually delightful.

The first and biggest problem you'll face is finding a jewelry designer, artist, or craftsperson whom you can work with. A regular jeweler will occasionally design and handcraft a ring and most of the prestige jewelers have "custom made" departments. Both these outlets of design will be expensive. The prestige store will charge you an incredible bundle and jewelers might too, since the designing and crafting of jewelry is out of their usual line of work. Some lesser known and mostly young jewelry designers are springing up in metropolitan areas, trying to establish shops or studios. They may be listed in the yellow pages of the telephone book under "Jewelry Designers." And then again, they might not be listed anywhere.

Through personal experience and the related experiences of friends, the author recommends that you find an artist or craftsperson who specializes in jewelry design. It seems that artists who can make custom jewelry are hidden away in abundance in most of the larger metropolitan areas of the country. They don't do a lot of advertising so it does take some looking around to come up with the right artist for you. How?

Check out craft shows. Usually several jewelry makers will be there displaying original wares.

Look for jewelry you like in boutiques that specialize in non-manufactured goods. Ask the merchant for the name of the person who makes the jewelry. He or she will probably tell you.

Call up the nearest college or the art department of the nearest university. Ask for the jewelry design department. If they don't have such a department, then hope that the dean of the art department can give you a referral. If you don't succeed at first, try another college.

Ask any craftsperson whose work you respect. Often fine-crafts people know other fine-crafts people in a variety of fields.

The last bet is jewelers. They sometimes know of local artists whose work is too "far out" for them to handle.

Once you do find an artist who designs and makes original jewelry, you don't have to assume that he or she is the only one that will give you what you're looking for. Ask to see a portfolio of photographs or sample pieces. Ask in particular if he or she has ever made wedding rings and if yes, ask to see those. If you want to level and tell the designer that you don't know much about the field and want to look around first, chances are that he or she will give you names of some fellow artists. Most craftspersons are pretty open.

Once you've decided on the designer, set a time when the three of you can meet for a long, relaxed session . . . over a drink in the local pub, in a park. Describe what you're looking for even if your idea is vague. Make any specific wishes clear. The designer should be able to follow your specifications (unless they violate aesthetic sense). If you're uncertain about what you have in mind and are open to ideas, make that clear. Someone involved with jewelry design should be able to sketch something along the lines of what you want. Work with the sketches; toss around ideas; modify or expand.

Working with a good designer is exciting. The three of you

can conceive a ring that will represent your own selves and your own love. It's a very special experience.

Have the designer quote you a price along about now. It's hard to be specific about the actual cost which will probably depend on materials. The price of gold, for instance, can escalate daily. Do insist on a minimum and a maximum quote. Write up an order agreement with a copy for each party. Fussy, but necessary, in case of misunderstanding.

Then, on a technical level, the designer will take your ring size. He or she will make up a wax mold of what you have decided upon and when the mold is finished you will meet again to try it on. The designer will determine that the mold fits exactly and that the design looks as the three of you had anticipated it would. If you agree on the mold, the designer will cast it, using a process that destroys the mold forever. You have a one-of-a-kind possession.

About Costs

There are a number of factors influencing the price of a ring made by an artist/jewelry designer/craftsman compared to one purchased through a jeweler.

First, there is the weight factor—the amount of gold used in a ring. The commercial jewelers have a more or less standard weight limit regardless of design. Jewelers cannot afford to use a "heavy" weight of gold in their rings because the markup they would have to charge on the real cost would make the ring prohibitively expensive. The jeweler has an overhead to maintain. This is why there are so many slender rings on the market. People have been encouraged and finally conditioned to accept the narrow bands and slim tiara settings since it would be too costly for the jeweler to push any other kind of gold jewelry. Slender rings—especially for women—have become the vogue. Indeed, they are the mark of femininity in rings—a tradition that is not coincidental in its commercial convenience.

A jewelry designer tends to put design first and then tries to skimp on metal if necessary. For instance, if the amount of metal used to construct a particular design would make the ring more expensive than a client planned to pay, the designer might scrape minuscule units of gold from the inside of the ring, lowering the weight. The jewelry designer's ring still may cost less or more. If it costs less, it is probably because the designer had no, or low, overhead and his or her profit percentage was under the usual commercial figure. If it costs more, it is probably because there is more material used in the ring's construction and, despite the lack of overhead, gold is incredibly expensive.

On this line of thought, comparing a wedding band that costs $80 from a free-lance jewelry designer and one that costs $80 from a commercial jeweler, you'll find that the designer's ring may be worth $40 in real cost while the commercial jeweler's will be worth $15 to $30. Custom-made jewelry can be a better buy.

Commercial jewelers, however, can afford to give you a better buy on traditional wedding bands or "standard" diamond rings. Their costs are cut by the fact that each style of ring or setting is produced at least by the gross and more likely by the thousands. If your desires are traditional, then the commercial jeweler is still your best source.

Possibilities

The family jewels:

If there is family jewelry offered to you by either of your families, feel free to accept with multiple thanks. If you like the jewelry, it could mean the rich tradition of a continuing heirloom piece or it could mean the start of one of your own traditions. However, accept on tactful conditions.

If you don't care for the setting, make sure that there will be no hard feelings if you have the ring reset. A commercial jeweler or jewelry designer could give it a whole new life without marring the historical heritage of ancestral fingers. Use your intuition to discern if there are any strings attached.

Accept if the ring once belonged to someone you love or someone who is a significant part of your ancestry. Your Great-Aunt Mildred's wedding ring from her second marriage may not do much for your own sense of tradition.

At turning points, such as marriage, families can come up with rare surprises and heartfelt generosity. Obtaining a ring, or a gem for a ring, in such a way is a warm and lucky start.

Estate Jewelry Stores

Estate jewelry stores buy out old jewelry from auctions and the closed estates of deceased or bankrupt persons. They have a wide range of jewelry, usually watches and gems. If wearing a "used" wedding ring doesn't bother you, then check here. Prices are lower. Styles vary from some genuine antique pieces to rings of the recent past that are just twenty years too old for fashion. You might find what you've been looking for—it's worth a try. Don't forget that if you find a good buy on a gem you like, you can have it reset to order by a jeweler or have it designed in an original ring by a jewelry designer.

Antique Jewelry

If you're not crazy about either commercial jewelry or contemporary jewelry, you might consider an antique look. You could track down a beautifully crafted "turn of the century" wedding band or a semiprecious stone in antique setting. Antique rings can be a reasonable find or can demand a high price for their age value, all depending on the age of the ring, the place of purchase, and the condition it is in. It's not a great idea to put a large amount of money into an antique piece. You have less assurance of quality here than anywhere else. Look for a carat stamp inside the ring. It may be there or it may have worn away. For a wedding band or a ring under $100, however, your purchase in an antique store could mean finding exactly what you've been looking for.

Museum Jewelry

Recently museum shops and jewelry stores have been selling handsome replicas of ancient rings. If an Egyptian pharaoh's ring strikes your fancy, then buy the best version available. The prices involved are not unreasonable—some are downright inexpensive. Check for gold content.

Engraving

Why not have the inside of your ring engraved with something personal. Many modern rings are so slender that they usually only bear a brief date or a few initials. Even so, some engraving is better than none, for identification purposes as well as sentiment.

Research for this book unearthed some wedding ring inscriptions that date back to the 1600s. From the Middle Ages to the close of the seventeenth century all betrothal rings were thick enough to be engraved with some sentiment. Often the thought was religious or lofty. Sometimes it was more basic. For example:

> "Sue is bonny, blythe, and brown
> This ring hath made her now my own."

The inscriptions, which were often lengthy, had a bad habit of rhyming. Following are some of the shorter sentiments which you may find quaint and perhaps even usable.

Love and live happy. (1689)

My promise past shall always last.

This and the giver are thine forever.

Joye without ende.

In loving thee, I love myself. (Very psychologically sophisticated!)

Love me and be happy.

Time lesseneth not my love.

I lyke my choyce. (The author's favorite.)

The best one of all is the one you make up—in prose or code or whatever you want. Look up "Jewelry Engravers" in the yellow pages and take your ring there to have a personal message engraved inside. It's the finishing stroke that makes your wedding ring entirely your own.

5. NEW WAYS TO "REQUEST THE HONOUR OF YOUR PRESENCE"

Wedding invitations used to be boring and alike: black and white engraved heralds with formal wording and rigid format. Today, sending out the good word can be a far more colorful experience. Literally. The manufacturers of wedding stationery have come up with colors to make your eyeballs dance. Harvest golds and oranges, mauve, all manner of pastels, royal reds, greens and blues and knock-em-dead neons.

Color isn't the only news. Wedding invitations are being printed on deckle-edged parchment paper, simple cards with colored borders, or floral and Florentine decked stationery. The usual fold-open kind are alive with geometric designs, flowers (daisies are big), and colored "sensitivity" photos of young couples walking hand in hand through the mist. The couple to be married can have their pictures put on the invitation cover or they can opt for their favorite quote or their initials in a heart. Invitations are made of every weight and texture of paper stock including metallic and velor papers, thick, transparent simulated parchment, and recycled paper. Tassles, embossing, gold leaf, and marbleized or enameled envelope linings are part of the pickings. They fold out, over, or open shutter-fashion.

In short, there is an incredible array where there was once only white vellum fold-out cards. It must be said that this inexhaustible variety contains a large amount of chaff with the wheat. Some of the invitations are downright abominable. But if you're looking for a nicely designed, colorful invitation, you're in luck. At last they can be found on the open market.

The invitations of which I speak must be ordered from a supplier who will print them. Most of these suppliers provide retail stores and print shops with a bulky sample book of stationery styles, designs, and type faces. The prices in the sample book are the supplier's retail prices, and no store should charge you more. The vast majority of these invitations are printed by thermogravure. To explain that, we now launch into a very short course in printing.

All invitation printing can be divided into three processes:

Offset

The offset printing process is based on the making of a photographic plate. Almost anything that can be photographed can be used to make a plate and hence be printed by offset. This includes all kinds of type face, line drawings, photographs, or handwriting. Low-cost offset printing—the kind done at the local "quick print" shop—is sometimes dull and not as sharp and black as other methods. No offset printing is raised. If you run your fingers across it, you feel the paper, not the print.

Thermogravure

The thermographic process consists of sprinkling a resinous compound onto a vague, printed image. The image is then heated to fuse the powder. The effect is a raised surface of shiny printing. Within the thermographic process is a new electronic method called photolettering that makes possible fine-line detail. Photolettering enables thermographers to use fancy and finely connected type faces that could not be utilized with the ordinary process. There is a larger price attached to photolettering, but the type face may be interesting enough to make it worth a little more.

Engraving

Engraving is one of mankind's oldest methods of printing. The message is etched onto a copperplate using acid. Much work by hand goes into the engraving process as well as costly materials, making it the most expensive process of all. To add to the cost, the paper used for engraving must be heavier than regular invitation stock. Some die-hards swear that nothing can look as fine as a well-done piece of engraving. And it is undoubtedly handsome. But the newer thermographic process produces printing that most people can't tell from real engraving. (To keep you abreast of the techniques of snobbery, the way to tell real engraving is by turning over the invitation and looking for indentation marks around the lettering, caused by the pressure of the copperplate.) So who cares? As a bonus for having your invitations engraved, the printer will usually give you the copperplate. The plate reads backward, making it a dubious keepsake.

If you're ordering three hundred flyers for invitations that you plan to hand out on the street corner, see a nearby "quick print" shop. As for something more formal, local offset printers can print invitations for you at a slightly more reasonable price than the thermographer. However, they will take just as long as the thermographer because they must send out for the type face you choose and must order the invitation stock as well. Since offset printers don't specialize in wedding invitations, they have fewer of the new styles of stationery to choose from. And, as mentioned before, the printing itself may be less sharp and will not be raised. For all these reasons, some offset printers carry the thermographer's sample books themselves and will send in your order for you just as any department or stationery store will. Incidentally, the wedding with the three hundred flyers was a big success. Family and friends were invited individually, and anonymous guests numbered about thirty-five.

Wherever you order invitations, remember that the salesperson who takes your order is just that—an order taker. He or she usually has a wealth of knowledge about the standard procedure for the traditional wedding invitation and is somewhat skeptical if you come up with a more original idea. The worst of these salespeople are very uptight about your innovations and act as if you are threatening all their acquired knowledge and their very job. Don't be intimidated. You can suffer them or you can take your business elsewhere. Happily, there is a growing number of stationery salespeople who find the individualized invitations fascinating and can often suggest some innovative ideas of their own.

Debunking Old Rules

The basics an invitation must include are: who is going to get married, on what day of the year, at what time and at what location? All else is extraneous.

The etiquette rules for invitations have both hampered the basic information necessary to some weddings and at the same time have added extraneous lineage. For instance, it is an etiquette-wise taboo to include the address of the church in which the ceremony will be performed. This seems a senseless rule, inconsiderate to visitors from out of town. On the other hand, proper invitation form insists that the year of the wedding must be spelled out in writing. Everyone knows for certain that the wedding will be held in the same year the invitations are issued—or in the case of December-mailed invitations, in the upcoming January or February. Yet the year always is included, written out in words lengthy enough to take up an entire line of space.

For some reason the traditional invitation finds it embarrassing to utilize anything so brash as a numeral. Even though

Saturday, August 16th at 8 P.M.

does as much mileage as

Saturday, the sixteenth of August
nineteen hundred and seventy-six
at eight o'clock in the evening

Another etiquette-book "don't" is printed response cards. Since most people are not going to R.S.V.P. in formal fashion, there seems to be no truly accurate way of keeping track of the number of wedding guests short of response cards. What's *wrong* with a response card? Actually, it's a thoughtful way to ease the guest's responsibility of replying to a formal invitation. Most important, it's a necessity if food is being served to a large number of guests. Most stationers are disregarding the uppity ban on the helpful little response card. You should too if its function and formal nature apply to your wedding.

What can be said about the traditional inner envelope and the delicate tissue insert except that they are useless leftovers from another era? In fact, they are decorations of that era, included to make the invitation more appealing in the same way that a quote or a tassel is included on today's invitation. Tissues once were supposed to "protect the engraving." One stationery salesman recently commented that now his young customers throw the tissue papers away or keep them to clean their sunglasses. The inner envelopes are still being sent out with the invitations for want of something better to do with them, seeing as how their flaps have no glue. But their time is growing short. Like all other natural resources, paper is becoming scarcer. Contemporary invitations ordered from a thermographer don't include the inner envelopes. If tissues and inner envelopes come automatically with your invitations, you may choose to use them or not. Nobody will care much either way.

The real news about wedding invitations is their new found flexibility in wording. Although "requesting the honour of your presence" is still rampant, there are any number of ways to reword the invitation and still include the basic information. You can say practically anything on an invitation that's applicable to being invited to a joyous celebration. A young clerk in a print shop commented: "You'd be surprised how many brides fall back on the formal wording just because they can't think of anything else they want to say." If that's true, it's inexcusable and very sad. There are many nifty ways to invite friends and family to your wedding.

Parent-Announced Invitations

The two main categories of invitation wordings are parent-announced and self-announced. Although all invitations used to be parent-announced (or in the absence of parents the closest relative available), more couples are finding it reasonable to issue invitations in their own names to their own wedding. Even so, a wedding has roots in the heart of the family and there's nothing clumsy or old-fashioned about acknowledging one or both sets of parents. Parent-announced invitations have a new way with words, too. For example:

*Our joy will be more complete
if you can share in the marriage of our daughter*
Betty
to
Harold M. Wrigley
on Saturday, the tenth of May
nineteen hundred seventy-six
at two o'clock in the afternoon
St. Paul's Methodist Church
Wilburville, Illinois
Mr. and Mrs. Oliver B. Boop

This invitation spells out the date rather than using the more concise numerical forms. Invitations sent in the name of the parents tend to gravitate to the traditional spelling-out procedure and in this case it works well. Since there are only two churches in Wilburville, one of them being St. Paul's, it was unnecessary to give a street address. Another example:

The most joyous of occasions
is the union of a man and woman
in celebration of life. . . .
Mr. and Mrs. Phillip R. Hammond
invite you to share in the ceremony
uniting their daughter
Pamela Leslie
and
Roger Van Pelt
Friday, November 5th at 8:00 P.M.
The Ethical Society
122 Union Street
Lexington, Kentucky
A reception follows the ceremony

Parent-announced invitations are now sometimes sent in the names of both sets of parents. This makes sense since two families are involved in the exchange. Guests of the groom's family who know nothing of the bride's parents will recognize the invitation as coming from friends. Unfortunately, this sensible idea is complicated by parents who feel that if they alone are paying for the wedding, their names should be the only ones on the invitation. If you can get around all that, the following wording is a good one:

Mr. and Mrs. Dominic G. Montague
and
Mr. and Mrs. Joseph S. Capulet
invite you to share in the joy of
the marriage uniting their children
Juliet
and
Romeo
This celebration of love will be on
Saturday, the fourteenth of May
at one o'clock in the afternoon
Cathedral of the Saints
Verona, Italy

The traditional method of centering the lines on the invitation is also open for new interpretation. Paragraph form makes the invitation look less like a formal announcement and more like a personal letter.

Please join our family in celebrating a
day of genuine happiness on Sunday, March the
tenth, at one o'clock in the afternoon at
Temple Israel, Cos Cob, Connecticut, when our
daughter, Donna JoAnn, will be married to
Mark Lipton Stevenson.

Your presence at this celebration of love
will be of special importance to all of us.
Carl and Helen Winters

Another paragraph format:

*Our daughter, Scarlett, will be married
to Rhett Butler on Friday, the 19th of June,
at seven o'clock in the evening.
    Their vows will be spoken at Trinity Episcopal
Church, 469 Peachtree Street, Atlanta, Georgia.
    We invite you to worship with us, witness
their vows, and be our guest at the reception and
buffet which will follow at Tara Hall.*

Mr. and Mrs. Frank P. O'Hara

Wording can be centered, flush, or set in a staggered combination of the two. One of the most attractive lines of stationery available offers wedding invitations printed on colorfully bordered cards. The cards are about 5″ x 7″, the inks are any color you choose, and the envelopes are lined to match. For a well-designed look on the card, new formats have been adapted—formats that would work well for any invitation.

*Mr. and Mrs. Whittier P. Hough
want you to share in their happiness
and join them when
Janet Hough Manning and Kevin B. Thurston
will be married
Saturday, April 6th at 2:00 P.M.
St. James Courtyard
near Third and Pine Streets
Philadelphia, Pennsylvania*

OR:

> *Nichol Gerauld and Brian Loft Mason*
> *want to go through life together*
>
> *Mr. and Mrs. Emil Loft Mason*
> *invite you to the wedding*
> > *Sunday, July 9 at 4:00 P.M.*
> > *the grape arbor at*
> > *12 Far Ridge Lane*
> > *Carlton, Oregon*

OR:

> *Suzanne and Paul*
> *are in love*
> > *Join us at the wedding of our children*
> > *Saturday morning, October twentieth,*
> > *at eleven-thirty o'clock.*
>
> > *First Congregational Church*
> > *West Oak Grove, Massachusetts*
>
> > > *Mr. and Mrs. Michael T. Long*
> > > *Mr. and Mrs. Knut Larson*

Innovations such as shown in these samples, or any others you have come across, can be mixed and matched to come up with an invitation that you and your parents will be pleased with.

Self-Announced Invitations

If you are paying for the wedding, you are free to issue wedding invitations in your own names. Even if you're not providing all the funds, you may issue your own invitations if your parents approve and sometimes even if they don't approve. The point to consider is whether anyone close to you will be seriously hurt or angered by your act. If yes, you'll have to estimate the consequences of the hurt and anger, consider other compromises, or somehow make the proposition unabrasive enough to cause minimum fuss.

If the wedding guests will be made up mostly of your friends, with a sprinkling of relatives, then it does make sense for you to send the invitations in your names. If the wedding is to be a large one with many of your parents' friends attending, then it might be reasonable to use one or both sets of parents to announce the invitation.

Self-announced invitations can follow any of the characteristics of the parent-announced kind or they could be something like the following:

ELIZABETH BARRETT and ROBERT BROWNING
The special day of our marriage is
December 13, at 8:30 P.M.
Howland Chapel, Unitarian Universalist Church
Cottage Street, Meriden, Connecticut
We hope you will join us for this happy occasion
and celebrate with us after the ceremony
at the home of Dr. and Mrs. Q. Gilbert
Easton, Connecticut

OR:

Edwin John Ransom
and
Sophia Cacciatore
will be married
Sunday, May 26th at 3:00 P.M.

*Come share in the
wedding celebration held
at the center fountain in
Washington Square,
New York, New York,
and the picnic afterwards*

OR:

*The most joyous of occasions
is the union of man and woman
in celebration of life . . .
come celebrate before God and nature
the marriage of
Tracy Joan Johnson
to
Derrick Laudermann
Friday, August 17th
at 4:30 in the afternoon,
Bear Creek Nature Reserve,
Hot Springs, Colorado*

OR:

*Irene Robling and Richard Bonds
invite you to share with us
the joy of our marriage
Sunday, the first of August,
at nine o'clock in the morning.*

*The home and garden of
Judge and Mrs. Frank McGinty
68 Freedom Road
Chicago Heights, Illinois*

These invitations are more or less straight. They are a fresh variety of the older wording but they're by no means the last word. Feel free to create your own completely original wording. Just make sure it's right for you and appropriate to the occasion and then go ahead and use it. Invitations derive their *raison d'être* from the messages they convey. Whatever you choose to do, make sure that the informative points of the message are clear.

When you order invitations from the thermographer, prices vary greatly with style and quantity and with extras like colored ink and lined envelopes. Watch for hidden costs. There's plenty of small type in the order books and it sometimes can catch you on such unexpected items as: "Wording in paragraph form—$10 extra."

In the face of economy a simple invitation using original wording can cost very little and look very personalized. One order book has a line of plain, regular-sized white or ivory invitations with a choice of any of the regular thermographic type faces (but not photolettering). The cost is less than $25 for one hundred. Without using any colors or decoration they can be as distinctive and individual as the wording and the format you have printed on them.

Making Your Own Invitations

If your wedding is small, you can always send handwritten notes as invitations. According to Emily Post and friends, a handwritten note is the most flattering invitation of all. Set an upper limit of twenty-five or thirty for handwritten notes —more than that will give you a royal case of writer's cramp. Split the note writing between the two of you and select some special stationery. Sending out wedding invitations on a sheet of your good old yellow-lined legal pad is calculated unpretentiousness. If you're keeping it casual, you might include your telephone number to make it easy for your guests to call in their response. Or you might not care about the responses at all if the wedding is small and the number of guests predictable.

You could design invitations and have them printed at the offset print shop. When designing your own, the number of options open to you is almost hard to handle. Here is what some couples did in co-operation with the offset printer:

Doug and Mary found out that they could order wedding invitation stock from the printer. They ordered seventy-five pale blue invitation cards and envelopes. Then they cut a sheet of white paper to the exact size of the cards on which Doug wrote the wording of the invitation in his own handwriting with a black-felt-tip pen. (For good reproduction you must use black ink—not a ball-point pen or any other colored ink.) The handwritten invitation was printed by the offset process on the front cover of the blue invitation cards. It looked natty and original. The whole cost was about $22.

Lyn and Larry tried a more ambitious project. They bought a ream of gold-colored textured paper from a local art-supply store. While they were there they picked up several sheets of transfer type in a script face that they both liked. Lyn made up the sample invitation, pressing the transfer type onto a white piece of paper cut to the same size as the oblong gold sheets. She left a large open space at the top. They took their gold paper and the sample to a printer and had him run it off in dark brown ink. Now they had 144 invitations printed in brown ink on gold paper with a large space at the top. Lyn had done a nice job with the type and it looked almost as if it had been set at the typesetter's. For the handmade part of the invitation, they bought two wood-block prints, carved in India. Larry chose one that was the shape of a single paisley and Lyn's was a circle with a delicate design carved inside. With rust-colored ink and rollers they spent a long afternoon together hand printing their wood-block designs on top of the invitations. The results were spectacular.

They needed about 100 invitations and of their 144 printed sheets, 103 turned out perfectly. They bought brown envelopes and sent the invitations out. Cost: About $50.

Bob and Carol combined invitations printed at the thermographer's with an original drawing printed at the offset shop. They ordered 150 invitations, envelopes, and response cards with the invitation message printed on the inside of the large ivory cards. Bob, a good artist, did a special pen-and-ink drawing which they took to the offset printer's. They ordered 150 drawings printed on a parchment-like paper which they supplied to the printer. The printer trimmed the drawings to the correct size and Bob and Carol centered them on the cover of each invitation, fastening the sheet at the top with a thin line of paper cement. Cost: $80. (Incidentally, if no one you know can draw, there are many pen-and-ink drawings in the world of fine art that you could "borrow" for your invitation cover. Check out the line drawings of Picasso, Matisse, or even Peter Max. If you'd like to invest in an original piece of artwork for your wedding invitation, consider commissioning a free-lance artist in your area to do an appropriate pen-and-ink drawing.)

Another couple ordered fifty plain invitations from the thermographer with the message printed on the inside. A mutual friend of theirs had a dark room setup in his basement and he agreed to help them. He printed a batch of photos of the couple walking along the beach. It was an appropriate shot since the wedding was going to be held at the foot of a lighthouse. They pasted the black-and-white photos on the cover of the invitations and, as an extra touch, signed the bottom of each invitation. Cost about $40.

Every individually designed invitation represents a new idea, a more personalized approach. You'll discover that you can come up with numerous ways to vary your invitation. Even if you're content to order from the already designed new offerings available, you can still make your invitation speak for you in character as well as in message.

Wedding Pollution Warning

There is a whole grab bag of junk that can be ordered for a wedding, usually through the printer. Printed matches, cocktail napkins, plastic cocktail stirrers, cakeboxes, cellophane-lined wedding cake bags—all printed with the lucky couple's names and magic date. Like the book of matches reading:

"A Perfect Match"
Judy and Rudy
June 12, 1975

One catalogue for such assorted printed sundries urged prospective buyers to "have your guests' favors imprinted in silver with your names and date—then they'll remember to send you anniversary cards!"

It's all insane, ugly, and costly—with one possible benefit. It's funny. The two of you can thumb through a catalogue of this array and end up laughing into the night.

6. CLOTHES FOR THE OCCASION

The Traditional Bridal Costume

Music: "The Wedding March"
Announcer:
Younger than springtime, more beautiful than the most exquisite flower, the bride approaches on the arm of her father. Hers is a gown to float in gentle breezes, shimmering like morning dew, poignant, blushed in pink, soft-flowing, feminine, and ruffled. As romantic as being wakened by a kiss. This is the storybook bride with loving care from your local department store.

> *Adapted from a*
> *bridal fashion show*

The above is an excruciating sample of commercial purple prose. But even those of you who abhor its sugared tone will admit that the outfit worn on your wedding day is a very special piece of clothing. To some people it takes on the distinction of becoming the most important piece of clothing to be worn in a lifetime. An agonizing amount of thought and money can go into the purchase of wedding apparel. And for some people the concern with wedding clothes doesn't end with the wedding. Every major city has specialists—usually associated with a dry cleaners or a department store—who will clean and hermetically seal a wedding gown for posterity.

Until recently the gowns being saved for posterity looked amazingly alike. Minor seasonal or fabric variations were the only differences that kept one white lace bride from looking like another. Even the bridal gown buyer at a major East

Coast department store admits: "It did used to be that all brides looked alike. But many still choose that very traditional look."

And that's true. When it comes right down to the moment of decision in buying a wedding gown, most brides are moved by a gut reaction to "look like a bride." It's an image that is quite hard to challenge. Once a girl has spent hours of her childhood in front of a mirror with lace curtains bobbi-pinned to her hair, the "bride as bride should be" is reflected in her whole system of values.

"So many brides," the buyer reports, "still want the high neck and long sleeves. Long veils are more popular in our store than they've ever been."

It's no surprise that most people, no matter what their age, are more comfortable following traditional ways. If you can visualize yourself as a bride only in a long, white gown, then that's what you should wear.

Now, go out and price a few long white bridal gowns. Notice that somebody is making a bundle off that lovely tradition?

A regulation bridal dress can cost anywhere from $90 to $600 in an average-priced bridal salon or department store. Venture into a classier shop in a higher-priced neighborhood and you will pay anywhere from $250 to $1,000. This is a steep tag for any dress made to be worn only once—no matter how much it warms your heart.

(Incidentally, laugh at all people who say that a bridal gown can be "cut down" to be used for a fancy dress after the wedding. Even if you have the heart to cut the dress off, it always looks exactly like a cut-off bridal gown.)

A recent trip to a large and distinguished department store in Philadelphia revealed that there is something old and something new in the bridal department. The traditional floor-length, white bridal gown has acquired a little more personality. Although it is still very possible to buy an utterly predictable white gown, there are also new possibilities for sale. Soft synthetic fabrics now make lovely flowing gowns—heavy-glossed jersey is a particular favorite. The Victorian look with high neckline, ruffled yokes, and leg-o'-mutton sleeves appeals to certain brides. Sophisticated robe-like gowns appeal to others. You can find a two-piece gown with a plain underdress and a lace coat that serves as a train. Dotted swiss is a popular summer fabric and banded with a wide baby-blue sash is selling well for "country weddings." There is even a hint of deco and the thirties look.

Wedding whites vary in color from pure white to ivory to candlelight to outright beige. The selection at a given store runs about 50 per cent pure white, 50 per cent ivory or off-white. If you don't know which shade of white would suit you best, try both. A rule of thumb is that brownettes, dark blondes, and redheads look great in off-white, while pale blondes and dark-haired girls can best wear pure white. Like most rules of this type the exceptions are overwhelming. One fairly reliable observation, however: Pure white emphasizes every flaw in your complexion. If you have skin that is unpredictable enough to break out the day before the wedding, then consider the beauties of an ivory dress.

Color, too! Manufacturers are now daring to make gowns in delicate colors: imperceptible pink, barely visible blue. Sometimes the "color" is the pastel center of a white lace flower used in the trim. There are print gowns on the market —usually tiny flowers on a wealth of white background. And one has gone all out with deep purple ribbon trim.

It seems to me that the spring/summer gowns are more varied and a little less expensive than the fall/winter gowns. The winter gowns tend to be more intricate with lace and beading and more formal in design. Many more winter gowns have long trains, heavier fabric, and more detailed trim; hence, the price is higher. The summer gowns seem to take advantage of the newer fabrics, the bent toward pastels, the absence of the train, as well as a wider variation of design both formal and informal. It is easier to find summer gowns on the reasonable end of the price spectrum.

In a department store or a bridal shop, the buyer is often known as the bridal consultant. Sometimes these functions are assigned to different employees, but for the most part the "de rigueur" consultant is also the buyer—a highly experienced merchandising expert. Her opinion is far from being a non-prejudiced one. She has special interests to appease in her role as consultant—one of which is that she must sell the bridal wear she has stocked.

Bridal consultants are known to be forbidding types. The ones who habitat large, "name" department stores and exclusive bridal shops take a great deal of trouble to come across as authoritative, card-carrying spokeswomen of the upper classes. This intimidating approach usually prohibits brides (and particularly mothers of the bride) from questioning their directives. Of course, this stereotype isn't always true. But those brides who prefer to dress for their wedding in traditional style should be aware of pressure from interests who tend to profit from their decision to follow accepted standards.

If you will be dealing with a bridal consultant, it is best not to use the word "non-traditional" in your negotiations. The consultants either react with the devious approach or they become defensive. ("What do you mean non-traditional? We carry the latest line of gowns here for a beautiful wedding. . . .") Substitute "contemporary" to keep matters running smoothly and describe what you have in mind in explicit terms.

Most brides who purchase a traditional gown pay in the range of $125 to $350. The dresses in this "median" price range are enough alike to make it hard to account for the difference between a $150 dress and a $250 dress. (How many ruffles and seed pearls account for a $100 difference?)

In what other purchase would a consumer allow for such a wide price differential with no questions asked?

A prospective bride shopping with her mother in a bridal shop chose a $300 gown over a gown costing $205. The fabric of the two dresses was the same and the styling was quite similar. The bride chose the more expensive gown because it had a slightly different neckline (both, however, were high Victorian necklines) and because the trim on one pleased her more than the trim on another. She also chose the more expensive gown simply because it cost more. Although she would never admit it, this bride reasoned that the more expensive the dress, the more beautiful she would be on her "day of days." The bridal consultant agreed with her decision all the way. The mother of the bride voiced one small objection and then relented.

Saving money on a dress designed to be purchased as a wedding gown is not particularly easy. But one of the best ways to get around the high cost is to order the bridesmaid dress of your choice in white or ivory. This is a happy solution, because bridesmaid dresses can cost under $75 and they are often of more contemporary design than wedding gowns. Sometimes a bridesmaid dress is of identical styling as the accompanying wedding gown. You could find one with a halter neckline, a matching shawl, a knife-pleated skirt, or other features that are denied a demure bride in an imposing gown. With the recent "all white" weddings, most styles of bridesmaid gowns can be ordered in off-white shades.

Bridal shops and department stores have sales, as do any other clothing outlets. One of the best sales occurs when the large department stores sell their sample gowns in the spring and fall. Sample gowns are sold at 50 per cent of their retail price. One catch: Sample sizes are small sizes. Only Junior sizes 3, 5, and 7 or Misses size 10 need apply. Similar markdowns can be obtained for dresses that have been "shopworn." Realize, however, that it costs about $20 to $30 to have a bridal gown cleaned carefully and completely. Subtract that from a savings on a soiled dress. Slightly soiled gowns that you can "touch up" yourself are fair game. So are gowns that need a small amount of hand sewing (ripped seams, zippers, hooks and eyes).

The savings on summer gowns have already been mentioned. If you have long-term plans for a wedding in the fall or winter, look over the summer crop of gowns carefully. Chances are that you'll find one that is just right for fall or even winter. Prices will be slightly lower; selection will be more exciting.

When you purchase a gown, ask about the cost for any alterations and hemming that need to be done. Dresses often need some alteration or hem change and bridal departments almost always charge for this service. If the work is any more exacting than routine, the charge may be considerable. Find out *before* the gown is purchased. If you think the charge is high, call a recommended seamstress or tailor and ask what she or he would charge. Alterations and hemming are customer services—the fees for such services should be low to nominal.

A money-saving long shot: Look up a bridal-wear wholesaler in the yellow pages of your telephone book. Don't call first; just go visit. Show up on the doorstep and ask if there are any miscellaneous numbers around that you could have a look at. Many wholesalers do have random gowns that have been returned or were miscounted on an order. They will sell them to you wholesale—hopefully. But if they do, they're doing you a favor. Selling wholesale gowns to brides off the street could ruin their status if the word got around. What store will buy from a wholesaler who is undercutting the store's own business?

A bridal veil usually finishes off the traditional wedding costume. Because it is almost a unique item of apparel in our society, the veil has come to stand for the role of the traditional bride.

Bridal veils have gone in and out of popularity, but at this point in history most brides following traditional dress choose to wear some sort of veil. The veil itself is interwoven with origins and symbolisms that are ever open to new interpretation. The veil concept involves such matters as: protection from the evil eye, modesty, guarded purity, and outright giftwrapping. (In ancient Rome it was the custom for the bride to wear a full-length veil that was saved to be used as her burial shroud. A not-too-festive touch.)

Veils in the department store and bridal shop are priced from $25 to $500. Some brides pay as much for a veil as they pay for their dress—occasionally they pay more. The little seeded caps and organza bows that secure the veil to the head have always been uninspired. But they're still around. Thank God for the disappearance of the tiara or mock-crown headpieces which flourished in the 1950s and reigned on for a decade or so. The tiaras, which always slipped askew at some point during the wedding, tended to make brides look like five-and-dime princesses.

In place of a veil with headpiece, recent brides have been turning to mantillas, an elegant old favorite enjoying new popularity. The lace mantilla can be short (about shoulder length) or long (waist length or below). The most beautiful (and expensive) ones are imported from Europe.

Brides are often choosing to wear a traditional wedding gown while rejecting the wedding veil. Some wear flowers or ribbons in their hair, or a hat. Some wear no head decoration at all. Omission of a veil has been known to emphasize the beauty of a traditional wedding gown while simplifying the total look. It does help to remedy the bridal-costume clutter.

If You Think Traditional Wedding Dresses Are a Drag . . .

If you don't see yourself in a long white wedding dress, there is a good deal of historical American tradition to back you up.

In the 1700s, a bride simply wore her best dress to her wedding, no matter what its color. This was a practical approach since no expenditure need be made and the dress lived a useful married life as well. In fact, dresses for the specific purpose of being married in didn't appear until the 1800s and then they were not at all obligatory. Dressmakers used detachable sleeves when they made these early wedding gowns so that the dress could be adapted for use after the wedding. The color was not universally white. From the nineteenth century to almost the middle of the twentieth century, the preferred color was a light coffee shade which was thought to be more flattering than stark white. Gradually, the popularity of white increased. By 1930, wedding dresses had become single-occasion garments to be worn only once by the original owner. They also had become one-color garments.

In the late sixties and early seventies, bridal shops and department stores started providing options for the contemporary bride. Unfortunately, these stores are few and their locales are almost exclusively in the largest urban areas. New York City, that hotbed of individualism, has a number of stores of this type. Bridal "boutiques" carry designs that are mod, ethnic, Victorian, or cotton-casual Americana. The prices range from $50 to $120 for dresses of muslin, eyelet, gingham, seersucker, "tablecloth" lace, and gay flower prints. There is an assortment of wide-brimmed hats, trimmed and untrimmed, made from sheer woven material or natural straw.

A contemporary or non-conventional dress does not necessarily come with a lower price tag. Bonwit Teller's and other higher-priced prestige stores carry an occasional "odd" dress, such as a yellow print daisy dress with hand-rolled hem that sells for $800. The concept of a non-conventional bridal gown can work for the bridal industry, too, as long as the price will measure up to the industry's standards of opulence.

Within the past five years, buyers at even the prestige stores have begun to realize that some of the finest wedding apparel can be found outside the offerings of bridal manufacturers. Eleanor Robbins, at one time the chief consultant for Bonwit Teller's New York City bridal department, came to her job with a Ph.D. in psychology and an open mind. She dressed a barefoot wedding party in decorated skirts and peasant blouses and outfitted another wedding party in antique petticoats covered with fancy aprons. At one point she was investigating the possibilities of a tie-dye wedding.

Obviously, Ms. Robbins was getting her inspiration and some of her stock from sources more varied than Priscilla of Boston. In fact, when the occasion and the money warranted it, she ordered 'designer originals in white that were never intended to be bridal gowns. She tapped the talents of designers such as Geoffrey Beene, Oscar de la Renta, and Donald Brooks.

Even if your wedding dress will never see the interior of a name designer's office, Ms. Robbins has hit upon a very useful idea. A white dress is as right for a wedding as a white wedding gown. Most manufacturers of white dresses cannot charge the same price as manufacturers of bridal dresses. There is just no "once in a lifetime" sabotage to allow them to do so. And there are innumerable quantities of lovely long dresses—some white—that would be smashing dresses for a wedding day.

Ferreting out such a wedding dress should be easy. The trend toward long-length casual and evening dresses has established itself securely in all parts of the country. Every dress shop and dress department in the larger stores has a display of long casual and not-so-casual dresses.

Most of these dresses are in a price range of $40 to $110. They are widely varied. If you're looking for a white dress, you'll certainly find one, particularly if it's spring or summer. Don't overlook the natural colors, florals, or strong, clear solids. Most brides who are marrying for the first time choose to wear white. There is no edict saying that you must. If you hanker for an orange dress or a paisley dress or a natural linen dress, then that's what you should seek out.

Choosing the right dress in these instances is largely a matter of instinct. You may try on four dozen dresses before you find it. But the right dress is going to say so as soon as you put it on. Kate discovered a long, canary-yellow dress with white trim and was hit by that "God it's great" feeling when she tried it on. This wasn't the white wedding dress she had set out to buy. She put it back on the rack and spent all afternoon and evening thinking about it. The next morning, she went back and bought it. Kate's wedding was to be a more or less traditional small church wedding, and her family took a dim view of a bright yellow wedding dress; they didn't understand it right up to the day of the wedding. But it was obvious to everyone present that day that Kate had chosen an extremely attractive dress that was just right for her.

The Mexican wedding dress has provided a number of recent brides with an alternative type of wedding apparel. Mexican wedding dresses range from plain, rather rough cotton to fine, almost sheer batiste. The dresses have lace inserts, bands of openwork, or, in some cases, colored embroidery. Some styles are quite plain with no decoration but capsule-shaped ivory buttons along the front opening. The genuine kind are imported from Mexico, of course, but the style has snowballed so that American dress manufacturers have been producing some very attractive adaptations. All dresses of that genre have a simple, festive look that suits many brides.

They are generally low priced, which suits everybody. Boutiques in cities and college towns are selling them in big-business fashion.

Don't feel limited to dresses. Prowl around stores and boutiques with both a preconceived idea and an open mind. Remember to look in the hostess shop in the larger department stores and even in secondhand stores—if that's your kind of thing.

Separates are fine, e.g., a long or short skirt in off-white with a soft ivory crepe blouse. Consider the same outfit in a bright, clear color. Include a paisley sash, jeweled belt, delicately crocheted, knitted, or embroidered vest, or jacket, or any other personalized something that would add up to your very own wedding look.

A large piece of jewelry could be an important part of your wedding apparel. So could big organdy aprons or gingham pinafores or a fringed silk shawl.

What about caftans for both bride and groom?

In cool weather, look for a velvet anything, made of the richest velvet available. A hand-knitted dress could look great but so could any dress that was soft, brushed, or furry. Wide wool pants could do it, too.

In warm weather dispel the "cover up for virginity's sake" theory. You may want a halter dress, a strapless dress, or an openwork sun dress of some sort. Don't feel that you have to have a floor-length dress. Short dresses can be effective, too. If you somehow feel clumsy in a long dress (some of us do), or if your wedding is taking place on a climb-to-the-top rock ledge, then a short dress is a more comfortable idea.

Slacks and flowing pants are fine in most outdoor weddings or casual-situation ceremonies (although I think wearing dungarees at weddings is trying a little too hard to prove something to the rest of the world).

The Parlour is a tiny boutique in center city Philadelphia that designs and makes many of the clothes it sells. Its

dresses have a look of simple funkiness—a sort of Betsey
Johnson "Alley-Cat" appeal. According to Ann Shine, the
manager: "We sell a lot of dresses to get married in. I don't
call them wedding dresses or gowns because that brings to
mind the blown-up monstrosities offered in department
stores and bridal shops. We never play up a dress as a
wedding dress. Such dresses are mixed in with all the other
long dresses and when a girl finds it she has a sense of discovery." What kind of women shop at The Parlour? "All
kinds," says Ms. Shine. "Most of them are what you'd call
hip women. But no matter how hip they are, they all dream
of a wedding scene—just not the 'regular' one."

Two of The Parlour's recent sales of wedding apparel were
for two very different types of weddings. For an outdoor
wedding, a bride purchased a light, woven-cotton dress that
was a pale "natural" color. The dress was long, trimmed in
ecru lace, and topped with a little striped midriff sweater
that was blue with red and black touches. It was a very effective dress. Casual and perfect for an outdoor wedding, but
somehow "special." As Ms. Shine put it: "We try to put a
certain amount of reverence in the clothes we make."

The other wedding sale at The Parlour was for a rather
large Palm Beach wedding which sounded as if it would be
embellished with all the Palm Beach extras. The bride, with
her mother, purchased a pants suit of white crepe woven with
a floral motif. The style was loose, flowing and casual, belted
with a wide sash of the same material, and decorated with an
ivory brooch.

Boutiques such as The Parlour are delightful places to
shop. Their nooks are often filled with antique jewelry and
crocheted purses and are decorated with subtle "old" colors.
Brides who come to these stores are purposefully escaping
the conventional look, the bridal costume. Yet none of them
wants to face disapproval on her wedding day. They want to
look beautiful, in the way they feel that beautiful applies to

them, and at the same time avoid being thought of as "far out." Many brides will shy away from a truly avant-garde dress because of the "all-my-parents'-friends-will-be-there" fear. A dress from a boutique can be a reasonable compromise for these brides. They are being appropriate for the occasion without being cowed into the expected way of dressing.

The object in such cases is to find a dress that is both flattering, and right for the occasion and which also makes an affirmative statement about the bride. "A bride needn't be afraid of the non-conventional dress," says Ann Shine. "She should only be concerned that the dress looks charming on her and depicts what she is like. When on-lookers are charmed by the way a bride looks on her wedding day, who's to say, 'Look what she's getting away with'?"

So how do you judge what is right for the occasion? Are there no standards by which an individual can choose the right look for his or her wedding day? If you move away from the approved bridal costume, how can the appropriateness of wedding apparel be gauged?

Perhaps the key word is "romantic"—romantic with a small "r" interpreted in any of its nuances. If you're ever going to have a romantic moment in your life, now's the time.

What is romantic? Romantic does not necessarily mean dainty, nor does it mean white or pastel. It does not mean lace or sheer or gloved hands or veiled head or any of the rules of femininity that are dictated to brides. Romantic doesn't even necessarily mean flowers, though for most of us flowers are an obvious and beautiful way to express the romantic.

Romantic in its broad sense is a combination of love, unreality, and imagination. It is sentimental, erotic, fanciful, and visionary. Romantic may mean impractical—but it doesn't imply outlandish. Its appeal is to the heroic rather than the offbeat. To romanticize is to dramatize, glamorize, heighten, embroider, color. Exciting words, these. Far bigger and more colorful than the white-and-silver wedding concept.

Romantic can be formal or informal. Indeed, today's clothes have shortened the distance between formal and informal. Formality has been stripped down, as the concept of "special clothes for special occasions" has been eased.

What all of this illustrates is the wide, wide range of choices open to the contemporary bride.

At a spring fashion show the theme was billed as "Up the Seventies"—a look at fashion to come in this decade. Several bridal outfits were shown—one with a headpiece that lit up and another that was bare-breasted. (To be worn by the flat-chested only, the commentator noted!) But all this seems far away and quite unfeasible as of the moment.

For now, the possibilities are up to you. At a May wedding held in the park, a bride wore a very successful dress that she had concocted by trimming a long, white antique nightgown and adding a handmade shawl. She looked just lovely.

Making It on Your Own

A really fine solution to the bridal gown lies in the power of the needle and thread. A bride who designs and/or makes her own wedding dress can incorporate the styling she likes with the fabric she chooses and tie it all together with her own selection of trim or decoration. Not only will the outfit have the mystique of an original, it can be made to fit perfectly and can cost a maximum of one quarter to one half of a purchased bridal gown. Figure that ingredients for a handmade dress should never total more than $70. (And $70 includes some pretty fancy fabric and trim.)

More important than the bonuses of choice and fit and cost is a certain creative involvement that comes from making your own dress. It gives you a sense of "designing" your wedding rather than finding yourself being put through the paces of "doing" a wedding. A surprising number of people agree: In 1970 over 500,000 wedding dresses were handmade.

Don't reject the handmade dress idea if you can't sew or don't like to sew. If you can't sew the dress yourself, someone who knows what they're doing can. You still have the power of design.

Where to start? Probably the best approach is to first look at fabric. You may or may not have a certain style of dress in mind, but the knowledge of what material there is to work with will certainly widen your ideas. The fabrics available for home sewing are just fantastic, particularly the synthetic fabrics of recent years. The stars of this show are the nylons and polyesters: lightweight, heavy, woven, or knit. Fabrics like Qiana, with its silklike luster, or smooth Lute Song would make great wedding dresses for either winter or summer. Crepe has become a more workable, handsome fabric since being made from polyester. So has chiffon. All the non-bonded stretchable knits offer themselves for flowing, clinging dresses, and the rich, heavy nylon jersey found in commercial gowns is available by the yard.

The old favorites abound, too, particularly cotton in its many forms: piqué, batiste, dotted swiss, eyelet, embroidered organza. Sculptured and quilted cotton are heavy and make spectacular wedding skirts for cool-weather weddings. Velvet, wool, satin, and moire are other cool-weather possibilities. Silk is seasonless but is a bit diminished by the easy characteristics of the new polyester substitutes.

The selection of trims, laces, ribbons, and edgings available is equally as startling. It produces the candy-shop syndrome in some people. ("I'll take a half yard of that and two yards of this and . . .") Take your time in deciding on the final trim and stick to your original plans as to where it goes. It's possible to get trim happy and start trimming every edge and seam in sight. A minimum of restraint works out best, lest you look like a walking notions counter.

The decision of which fabric to buy shouldn't be finalized until you've juggled with the options of styling.

The four major dress pattern companies supply patterns specifically for bridal gowns and bridesmaids dresses. The patterns differ mildly—most are strictly traditional, not much different from department store fare. If they're what you're looking for, fine. But you don't have to follow the patterns as pictured on the page. First, a change of fabric from the one shown or an elimination of trim or the abolishment of an overskirt could change the look of the style entirely. Secondly, if you have some experience in sewing, you know how easy it is to interpolate patterns—the sleeves from one pattern, the neckline and bodice from another, a narrowed or widened skirt from a third. This is a fine way to come up with an original but it does take a bit of know-how.

You're not limited to the bridal-wear/formal-wear section of the pattern book either. Look around. Some of the designer patterns are unique and stylish—they can make exceptional wedding dresses with the right choice of fabric. The front feature section in the book, the regular dress section, and even the easy-to-sew section all contain ideas and patterns that you can put to use. In fact, if you are interested in a new look, skip the bridal section altogether. Bridal dress patterns are usually holdovers from editions long past. New bridal styles are introduced only infrequently—long dresses in the feature pattern section come out monthly.

If you have a favorite dress that has always fit just right, you could sacrifice it as a pattern for your wedding dress. Take it apart at the seams, iron the pieces out, and use it as a pattern to cut your fabric. A bride in Georgia did just that with the dress she wore the first time she met the groom-to-be. The old dress had been a long, country calico which she wore to an outdoor concert where she tried to ignore this obnoxious guy who was determined to talk to her. . . . The dress for her wedding day was an exact duplicate made in white Swiss cotton and trimmed with green ribbons.

There are many brides (a majority perhaps) who know for certain that they haven't the experience or the inclination to attempt sewing their wedding dress. If that description fits, you might want to consult a dressmaker and still retain your creative rights over what you will wear. The pluses are there. You can design your dress and choose the fabric and trim and expect a perfect, flattering fit. The cost will be higher than it would be if you sewed yourself. But it might still be lower than what you would pay for a manufactured gown. Add the maximum cost of materials, $70, to the maximum cost of the dressmaker, $110, and you've still beat the higher-priced gowns that most brides seem to wind up with.

Ah, the personal dressmaker, delight of rich women everywhere. And here you are looking for one. Word of mouth is still the best way to find a good seamstress. Chances are your peer group won't have the slightest idea of where to find a talented, reasonably priced seamstress. There are a few seamstresses of the underground variety who advertise in the local counterculture or college newspaper. But they are few in number. More likely, you'll have to ask your aunt or a neighbor or a friend of someone who knows such things. You can try the yellow pages of the telephone directory under Dressmaker, or you can check the personal services or work wanted columns of your local newspaper. Another possibility is the women who staff the alteration departments at large stores. Sometimes they do dressmaking on the side.

Once you've found your seamstress, take your patterns or your ideas to her and hear her out on them. Buy all fabric and trim yourself after you get her okay on the feasibility of working with your choices. She will supply notions. Agree on a price range and on a deadline when the dress is to be finished.

Some dressmakers are seamstresses and others are would-be

designers. If you've come up with one in the creative bracket, you might not need a pattern. Tell her what you want, she'll add to your ideas or modify them. The dressmaker takes initial measurements of your body on your first fitting. She then cuts and bastes the dress together. You return for a second fitting when she alters the dress to fit you exactly and makes any changes that seem to suggest themselves. The price for this kind of service varies widely. Dressmakers charge by the amount of time and the intricacies that go into their work, though they seldom actually charge by the hour. The cost for services will probably be over $50 and should be under $130. "Name" dressmakers run considerably higher. Cost of fabric, trim, and patterns comes out of your pocket in addition.

A word of caution. There is usually some female relative in your family who can "whip up a dress for you." Neighbors fall into this category, too. Make sure you have the greatest trust in the talents of the person involved before agreeing to such an arrangement. If your volunteer dressmaker is a professional or a near-professional, you are in luck. If not, you may be in for some hard feelings. Here is a true story: "My eighty-year-old grandmother spent the last three months making my wedding gown for me. Morning till night she bent over that dress. It looks like hell. Now, I have to wear it or she will go to her deathbed hating me."

Most art colleges and some art departments within universities have fashion-design programs. For a fair price you might be able to commission an earnest student to design and execute a wedding dress for you or wedding apparel for the groom. One student commissioned from an art college got absorbed with the project and designed a whole wedding party's apparel. It met with such approval that she herself had to hire a seamstress to help with the sewing. She charged the couple $100 plus materials and expenses and the promise of free photographs to go into her portfolio.

Suppose you decide that you can tackle the making of the wedding dress yourself. The first thing you'll need is plenty of time. It's a good idea to start the dress four months ahead of the wedding. That allows lots of time for errors or changes. Brides who are bent over the sewing machine two days before the wedding are inviting hysteria. Don't attempt making your dress if you have less than four weeks to work with.

Once you have the time, the fabric and the pattern—then what? Before plunging a scissors into your chosen material, make a mock-up of the dress first. This is a particularly wise idea if you are employing an original design or interpolating patterns. It eliminates fatal mistakes and insures perfect fit. Buy adequate yardage of cheap cotton or muslin in the bargain basement of the most cut-rate store around. The cheaper, the better. If you pay more than sixty cents a yard, you're buying the wrong stuff. Find a plain, pale color so you can best see the lines of your dress.

Cut out the dress from the pattern or patterns and baste the mock-up together. Using this model you can rip seams apart, adjust for fit, and then resew. Check any adjustments that are called for when piecing two patterns together. If the whole dress is disappointing, you have the option to start all over again with a better style. This process should take anywhere from two to four days of comfortable sewing spans. It is worth every minute it takes.

At this time, a reconnaissance mission to the bridal shop is legitimate if you're sewing a somewhat traditional gown. Tell the salespeople that you're just looking and then get a good look at the construction of the dresses on display. Check out how the underskirt may be sewn together with the overskirt at the hem or how they may be separately hemmed for more fullness. On sheer fabric, nylon horsehair braid may be used around the collar and cuffs as well as the hem. This braid may be used on opaque fabric as well to give gentle body and firmness. It is as easy to sew on as bias tape and eliminates the hand hemming of a full skirt. Find out how the darts and necklines of the gowns are finished. Look what they did to the zipper below the waistline on two-layer skirts. It all sounds complicated in writing. A hard look at the construction of some bridal gowns can put you at ease with the most fancy traditional styling.

The bride who is less inclined to be traditional gets free rein in sewing her wedding dress. She can make a dress that is slightly *nouveau*. Or, she can incorporate interesting materials and original designs for an individualized effect. At a spring daffodil wedding the bride made her dress from a large-size embroidered tablecloth. She designed it so the smaller-scale edging embroidery and lace were around the hem and the bottom of the sleeves. The center of the cloth with its larger lace detail was made into the bodice. The bridesmaids were in tablecloth dresses, too.

A wedding dress success with an ethnic look was made from a purchased Mexican wedding dress. The dress was plain, of light beige nubby fabric. The bride embroidered and appliquéd colorful designs on hem and neckline borders. The hemline border of flowers had her name and the groom's name worked in crewel yarn along with the date of the wedding. The result was a festive heirloom.

Handmade buttons of baked-ceramic material, shaped like hearts and painted bright red, ran down the front of a white eyelet dress for one wedding. Another bride in white had her dress dashed here and there with tiny pearl-white, baby-sized buttons.

A wedding which took place in October had both bride and groom in outfits made from hand-woven material that the bride had made over a period of a year. The fabric was medium-weight woven wool in loomlike shades of rose, purple, and brown. The bride and groom had the same shades in their fabric, but in different degrees of color and in different patterns of weaving. The dress and the shirt were of starkly simple design.

The sewing of wedding apparel need not be limited to the bride and her female attendants. Consider the possibilities for the groom. If he is going to be locked and suspended into a standard piece of rented formalwear, why not individualize his outfit with a handmade vest, tie, cummerbund, or shirt. The fabric stores are stocked with great material for the groom, too. Ties and cummerbunds can be made from any of the colorful materials that are lightweight and pliable. Vests, which need more body, look great made from raw silk, Ultrasuede, or sculptured cotton. For grooms without jackets, a flowing shirt made of Swiss handkerchief wool, challis, or linen would be a personalized and romantic project. Don't forget to see what the tapestry section of the fabric store holds for you and the groom. A bride from Colorado made her groom a Victorian jacket from fabric designed to upholster sofas. The fabric was a heavy beige cotton, quilted in a medieval design of black and brown. Nobody upstaged *him*.

Inheriting Family Wedding Apparel

Wearing your mother's or grandmother's wedding dress can add a deeply meaningful rite to your wedding. The same feeling comes with inherited veils, shawls, gloves, garters, and jewelry. Passed-on apparel is witness to a generation—perhaps two—coming full circle. It can give you a deep-rooted sense of yourself and a feeling for the factors and people that have brought you to this important point in your life. The relatives are guaranteed to cry.

Today, some old-style dresses are in vogue. Wearing your mother's 1944 wedding dress is going to make you look very savvy. Add some Carmen Miranda platform shoes, plucked eyebrows, and an angora sweater and you're a bride ahead of your time.

However, don't let anyone push you into wearing a dress, veil, or heirloom piece of jewelry. As tearful and touching as the bequeather may be, the item must be loved by you or it shouldn't be worn by you. This is where picking the "significants" in your life may cause some pain to your family. Be as kind as you can be, but stick to your own inclinations. The heirloom value of a dress or a piece of jewelry is not greater than the value of your own taste.

Indignation and hurt, if there are any, will roll off in a matter of days or weeks. (If the involved member of your family is elderly, give it more time.) Grudges at a wedding disappear faster than champagne.

Jill, who was married last year, knew there was going to be trouble over her grandmother's wedding veil. Her grandmother had died while Jill's mother was a teen-ager and the veil had been worn for sentimental reasons by her mother, her aunt, all her married female cousins, and her older sister. The veil itself was now yellowed and the headpiece was a cumbersome flat bonnet.

Jill's wedding dress was made of pure white textured cotton and it tied with a red sash. Anything made of net or tulle would spoil the look. Anything off-white or yellowish would distract from the dress's fresh whiteness. Jill wanted to wear a wreath of poppies and anemones in her hair and skip veils altogether.

Everyone in the family who had worn the veil wheedled and coaxed Jill. They called her on the telephone and wrote little notes and became more miffed and determined with each polite refusal. Finally her father stepped in and called off the guilt campaign.

At the wedding reception, her ancient great-uncle, the brother of her grandmother, cornered Jill and offered to tell her a secret. He whispered that he was proud of her for refusing the veil and he was a little disturbed that it had become such a family idol anyway. It seems that Jill's grandmother had ordered the veil through a mail-order catalogue and it had arrived just a few days before the wedding. The veil didn't look the way it had in the catalogue and grandmother didn't want to wear it. She wanted to wear flowers in her hair instead. Jill's great-grandmother would have none of that— her daughter must wear a veil pulled over her face as all proper brides did at that time. No veil, no virgin. What would people think.

Grandmother felt she didn't have a choice and since it was too late to send the veil back she wore it.

The old uncle had held his tongue as the veil had come to mean so much to Jill's mother and all the other relatives. He asked Jill to do the same, and she did.

Of course the other side of the story is that there are plenty of brides, and grooms too, who would give anything to find a wedding garment filled with family history in their attic.

A Main Line bride of long and blue-blooded heritage wore the Indian muslin dress that her maternal great-great-grandmother had worn at her marriage in 1845. The dress had a low neckline that traveled straight across from shoulder to shoulder, wide sleeves that gathered at the wrist, and a flowing skirt. Appropriately enough, the style of the gown is classified as being of the romantic period. Her wedding party wore dresses of yellow muslinlike cotton modeled after the bride's.

Another bride, married at a lakeside ceremony at the family's Adirondack mountain home, wore a white lace "summer dress" that had belonged to her grandmother and tied it with a wide sash of dark blue ribbon.

A "summer" or "boardwalk" dress from around the turn of the century can be one of the most beautiful dresses that a bride can inherit. These are white dresses of cotton batiste or light linen trimmed with inserts of cotton lace, embroidery, and Irish crochet. The styling is usually simple and the fabric and trim relationship intricate. Often these dresses will have high necklines and tiny tucks on a full bodice. In their day they were considered casual dresses, but they are certainly substantial enough and "fancy" enough to wear to your wedding.

Finding a garment with a romantic history may be easier than you think. However, restoring it to its original beauty may take a great deal of care and expertise. Time wears heavily on cloth. Fibers weaken, discoloration takes place, the body goes out of the fabric, leaving it thin and limp. Many of these signs of age may be remedied and others are past help. It's difficult to predict which clothes are beyond recall. You never really know if the garment can be restored until you try restoring it. Some of the most helpless-looking dresses from the turn of the century can be simply washed and ironed into splendid condition.

There are two initial rules for all garments rescued from posterity. First, never brush the dust from anything old. As tempting as it might be to "dust off" with hand or clothes brush, resist the urge. Brushing out dust in old fabrics is really only brushing it in and doing possible harm to the fibers. Dust, that nothing-looking substance, has plenty of cutting edges. Brushing it vigorously into the fabric could be the final strain for fragile fibers. Try any method that draws the dust out. One of the most successful is a hand vacuum cleaner—the small kind that is used on men's suits. Even the scrupulously cleaned nozzle of a regular cannister vacuum cleaner could be used. Or, you could fortify the garment, place it on a coat hanger, and secure it soundly to your clothesline on a breezy day. A gentle wind draws out dust harmlessly.

Which brings up rule number two: Fortify the garment before using any cleaning procedure. Fortifying means to reinforce important seams by hand sewing with needle and thread. Turn the garment inside out and sew right over the original seam, making a second line of tiny stitches directly over the first. Fortify any seam that will receive body stress, such as seams at the side, back, waistline, front, or bust. Of particular importance is the seam attaching the sleeve to the body of the garment. This seam receives more stress than any other. If the garment cleans well, you may also want to fortify the underarm with additional fabric.

Each dress will have its own cleaning problems in the restoration process, but there is one cardinal rule. NEVER, NEVER dry-clean old cotton or linen. It will yellow irreparably if it comes in contact with modern dry-cleaning fluids.

The best way to restore old cotton or linen is to use the old-fashioned method that kept the dress sparkling in its own time. You first start with a sunny day—as mild and bright as the current season allows. No rough winds. Your great-grandmother would call it "a good day for the washing." Fortify the dress and remove any dust. Then wash it by hand with hot water and pure detergent. (Ivory is best.) Bleach it very carefully with a mild bleach solution. You can put the bleach right in with the suds. Squoosh the dress gently with your hands, giving it two doses of suds and bleach if you think it needs them. Now comes the secret—rinsing. Rinse the dress until you think the effort is becoming ridiculous. Rinse it a dozen or so times. A little suds and mild bleach never hurt even the oldest fabric. However, bleach left to dry in worn-out fabric may be enough to make the brittle fibers shred. Rinse it once more just for good luck. Don't wring it out; bundle it up in a towel and let the terrycloth absorb the largest part of the moisture. Put your dress on a clothes hanger and secure it outside in the sunshine. Sunshine is still the finest bleaching agent anywhere.

Remove the dress while it is still damp. If it has dried out too much, sprinkle it liberally with water to achieve a "damp to the touch" feeling. Roll it firmly, jelly-roll fashion, wrapped in a towel (like boys roll up their swimsuits). Place it in the refrigerator for several hours. When the dress is damp and cool, it will press beautifully. (This is especially true for linen.)

Try pressing without any steam; just set the appropriate dial for cotton or linen. If the dress has embroidery or lace trim, press the trim on the wrong side with a thick towel underneath. This makes the trim stand out in relief, as it did on its first day of wear, rather than smashing it flat. Always press on the straight grain of the fabric. On most dresses that means press from top to bottom or vice versa. Never slide your iron from side to side across the dress.

To put body back in the dress (which is looking greater all the time), use some spray starch. Use it wisely—a squirt here and there—and watch the temperature of the iron. There have been more than a few bitter scorch stories in the historical annals of spray starch.

When you've finished, you have a wedding dress with real tradition. You could wear it as is or you could add your own touches—a wide, colored sash, an Indian mirror-work vest, a crocheted pastel shawl.

Lace has been a wedding staple for quite some time. Your chances of inheriting or discovering old wedding lace are good. Venetian, Valenciennes (Val), Milan point, rose point, Alençon, and English point are a few of the popular varieties used both now and in the past. Most laces are made from cotton or silk and most can be hand washed. (Though the cotton "does up" better.) No bleach should be used unless the lace is a very sturdy cotton.

The biggest hazard in washing is that old lace, when wet, can snag on just about anything. Wash the lace in a net bag or a pillowcase to prevent the delicate strands from breaking. Hang smoothly in the sun to dry, but do not stretch. If the lace is still too yellow, try a whitener that doesn't contain real bleach, and wash again. Hang again in the sunshine. If the lace seems to be able to take it, continue this procedure until the desired whiteness is achieved. Press on top of a thick fabric surface—a terrycloth towel would be fine—and for extra protection of very fine or very old lace, use a thin press cloth on top of the lace as well.

Restoring unwashable fabrics presents another problem. Heavy old silks and satins are tricky numbers which may do anything from run to dissolve in the presence of water. They are somewhat of a mystery to even the finest of dry cleaners. You need to find the most experienced and wisest dry cleaner around.

If you live within a reasonable distance of a museum—attached either to a city or a university—call or write or take the dress to the museum's curator of costumes and textiles. Ask this person where the museum sends its old, intricate dry-cleaning problems. They may not send them to anyone who performs such a service for the general public. If not, ask for recommendations of nearby cleaners who would be qualified to do the job. If no help is available, ask how you can approach your specific problem yourself.

If there is no source of expertise to call on, then seek out a local dry cleaner. Search for this dry cleaner in much the same way that you would search around for a reputable brain surgeon. Look up French dry cleaners in the phone book. Sometimes the word "French" is a meaningless come-on and sometimes it really does stand for the traditional hand-cleaning method of high excellence. Take your dress to this dry cleaner and present it to him with the gravity of signing him on to an international intelligence mission. Ask him how he will approach the problem. Get his opinion as to its possible success. Be aware that he must disavow responsibility for the dress if something should go wrong. He will tell you that beforehand. If he becomes too intimidated, ask him for the names of "higher ups" in the business where you could go to get the dress cleaned. When you finally have found the little old wizard of dry cleaners, leave your dress with him, go home, and pray.

You might be able to take some action yourself. If the area to be cleaned on your non-washable dress is small—spots or soiled cuffs and collars, for instance—you could use a blotting method. (This method was used in the fashion wing of the Philadelphia Museum of Art by the curator, Mrs. James McGarvey, to clean a display of non-washable samplers that had been embroidered by young girls of colonial times.)

Buy a large white desk blotter and cut it in half. Get a can of Renuzit dry-cleaning fluid. Lay the area to be cleaned over one half of the blotter and with a clean white rag apply the Renuzit to the dirty area. When the area is heavily moistened with the fluid, place the other half of the blotter on top and press. The dirt is soaked into the upper and lower blotters. This is a slow method, impractical for a whole garment, but it does a fine job on small areas. (Try a bit of the Renuzit on the inside hem or seam of the garment first. Allow it to dry so you can check for discoloration. There should be none, but with old fabrics you never know.)

A final word about the cleaning part of restoration. Although you don't want inherited wedding apparel to look soiled or dingy, don't give up if it never becomes pure white. Don't even give up if the results are a deeper ivory than you imagined. It's not supposed to look as if it came off a rack in the department store. The charms of the garment are its history, its inheritance, its quality of age. It should have enough priority to be worthy of plans made in deference to its age. Couple it with antique jewelry, yellow and amber flowers with dark foliage, the softness of candlelight. The garment may be important enough to you to warrant planning the whole wedding with a period look in mind—upswept hair, a velvet smoking jacket for the groom, a turn-of-the-century reception.

The restoration process of some dresses means alterations as well as cleaning. Our good ancestors were often smaller women than we. Less vitamin C and all that. If Grandmother's wedding dress is the equivalent of today's size 5 junior petite and you're the equivalent of a 5'8" size 13, there's not a whole lot anyone can do. Blame the vitamins.

If the fit is within reasonable range, however, simple alterations can be made. Usually these will deal with hems on sleeves and at the bottom of the dress, tucks, darts, side seams, and fasteners. On all these problems, work by hand and use a think-twice policy.

If letting down a hem exposes an indeliable "hem crease," sew some matching trim over the crease. If necessary, tint the trim in a weak tea solution to match the off-white color of an old dress. Same trim idea works for cuffs. If the cuffs and collar are too shabby, they can be replaced with duplicates of corresponding material or can be substituted with purchased trim or hand embroidery.

Baste all fitting alterations before sewing final stitches and, if possible, before opening original seams. Use the sewing machine at your own risk. Hand sewing is safer on garments older than forty years. Get alteration help and an extra hand for fitting from someone who sews. You could contact a seamstress in the same way you picked the dry cleaner.

Taking in seams and darts is a cinch, but, as already mentioned, work on older dresses usually goes the other, harder way. Letting out seams and darts is more difficult and "shows" on old fabric. Try to let out seams that won't be as obvious. For instance, to make the bodice larger, let out the side seams, which your arms might hide, before you let out darts on the front of the dress. Consider the possibilities of buying antique lace, embroidery, or other old trim and inserting as panels to add to a skimpy bodice or skirt. Regather tiny waistlines or insert elastic extensions to waistbands.

The dress might have an inadequate fastener system. Pre-zipper days highlighted hooks and eyes, snaps or weird buttons. Early zipper gowns feature heavy metal zippers, now showing their chipped paint. If possible, strengthen all weak systems with facsimile substitutes. Don't, of course, rip out a handsome long row of hand-covered buttons with loops. If the fastener system is secure, unobtrusive, and goes with the dress, then fortify it with needle and thread and accept it.

Fabric under the arms is the fabric that tends to deteriorate first. This is due less to perspiration than to the intense body heat in those particular areas and the tension on the fabric from the movement of the arms. You might want to fortify this area with fitted inserts sewn on the inside of the original garment.

What if your efforts don't pan out? What if the dress never quite makes it as the right dress for your wedding day? You could tuck it away for some other bride on your family tree or you could fit it into your wedding day apparel by less obvious, more ingenious means.

You might remake the dress. This is especially appropriate for dresses with large amounts of material that are still in good condition. It's just that the styling or the fit or some particular part of the dress is beyond all help. Take the dress apart, seam by seam, and using a pattern, cut a new dress from the old. Sew up your new style and you'll have made yourself an updated heirloom. (This method works well on the huge balloony gowns of the fifties with their yards and yards of skirting.)

If remaking is an impossible alternative, take the trim off the dress and sew it onto the wedding gown that you're making for yourself. Antique lace, and even not-so-antique lace, is as beautiful on a pure white gown as on a gown of ivory or some closer color. Pam made herself a long, simple dress of peach-colored crepe and sewed the old lace from her grandmother's wedding gown over the bodice and at the collar and cuffs. You could also put the trim on your veil, if you're wearing one, or use it as ribbon for the flowers you hold.

Perhaps you could use the skirt of the older gown as a petticoat underneath a wedding gown you've made or purchased. A mother of the groom, in Albany, New York, was deeply pleased when her new daughter-in-law did just that. The bride used the rather unspectacular taffeta skirt of her mother-in-law's wedding gown as an underskirt to the dress she made for herself. Her dress was made of a heavy satinish fabric and needed the support of the taffeta. It was a coup in dressmaking as well as diplomacy.

Clothes for the Mother of the Bride or Groom

Give Mom a break. If she plans to wear dressy clothes to the celebration, tell her to stay away from the "Mother of the Bride" section in just about all department stores and bridal shops. Dress manufacturers and retailers unabashedly soak the good woman for her child's wedding day. And besides being expensive, the typical mother-of-the-bride dress is really boring. For a price somewhere between $85 and $200, most bridalwear places will try to sell your mother a street-length jacket dress or coat dress made of silk shantung, brocade, or lined lace.

Clue your mother in on the fact that she can get a plain, conservatively cut bridesmaid's dress for a fraction of the price that a specified mother-of-the-bride dress would cost. Unless she is a size 44½ there's bound to be a bridesmaid dress she likes that can be ordered or altered to fit her. She can pick her favorite color, too.

The selection of the style is particularly important. If a flattering, non-cutesie dress is chosen, there is no way to tell that it's not being worn for its intended purpose.

Your mother probably will be delighted by this whole idea.

Wearing a bridesmaid's dress will make her feel much younger and spiffier than she would feel wearing all that deadly matron's wear.

If your mother prefers to wear a street-length dress, try to encourage her to wear one she already owns and loves. If she wants to buy a new dress, warn her about the bridal department and then assure her that anything she chooses will be just great. Mothers of the bride and mothers of the groom have a special reason to shine on their children's wedding day and they'll look best and feel best in clothes that please them. Even if your wedding is quite casual, let your mother wear whatever dress, white gloves, and/or hat she pleases. If you can wear what you want, so can she.

The society page recently ran a description of a wedding where all seemed to be going according to etiquette-book procedure. The bride was in a perfectly traditional bridelike gown; the bridesmaids were feminine and they all matched. Everything was in its place. Then the write-up took on a whole new note:

"The bride's mother wore red—a halter-necked American beauty knit polyester crepe. This was topped (at the church) by an English peasant print shirt and an antique paisley vest, which Mrs. Bates made from an old New England piano shawl. At the reception, she removed both shirt and vest."

Vive Mrs. Bates! The nervous society columnist is making sure to give her equally astonished readers all reassurances that Mrs. Bates was covered up at the church but stripped down at the reception.

Beyond the Ties of Black and White

So often it seems that the bride *is* the wedding, and the groom is merely present. He is a necessary, respected, principal figure and most often in this role he wears the necessary and respected garb of grooms everywhere. Unfortunately, a bride in an individualized gown is often accompanied by a groom tucked into his black and white tux. But things are loosening up.

Sometime in the sixties, the rentalwear business asserted what everyone has known for a long time—that men love to get dressed up for special occasions no more or less than women do. Ages past had their gentlemen dressed in embroidery, lace, and fine fabrics with no implied lack of masculinity. Fortunately, during the past ten years, colorful and decorated men's wear has re-entered the fashion picture.

More leisure time and affluence contributed to the return of "Fancy Dan." And there were other factors. Male singers, actors, and stage performers were spicing their acts with wild, colorful formalwear. Then there was the discovery and wide marketing of synthetic fabrics. The abundance of the synthetics, their lowered prices, and their unique adaptability turned the heads of the manufacturers of men's formalwear and the buyers of rented formalwear.

But the whole problem isn't solved yet. First, no matter what rented garments look like, they are still rented clothes. There is a deadening, gray impersonality to rented clothes. Here, on a very special occasion of your life, you are dressed in clothes that don't belong to you. They belong instead to a commercial interest that makes money by clothing all their customers in uniform fashion.

Then there is the lingering problem of style. The traditional styles can be a drag and the new colorful styles often look cheap and gaudy. The choice runs something like this:

An urban rentalwear shop sported the cheapest and gaudiest summer jackets seen anywhere. They were made from a drizzly textured, thin polyester material in lime, lemon, and apricot, with a heavy collar of coarse black velveteen. The idea behind the jackets represented the break-through in men's fashion. But the execution was shoddy, the styling was thoughtless, the effect abrasive.

On the opposite side of the store was row on row of the usual: black tails, tuxedos, cutaways, sack coats, and white dinner jackets. They're still in abundance with their gray-striped trousers and other colorless accessories. Some browns have invaded the territory and they are a handsome, warm addition, but the black-and-white imperative reigns.

When it comes to weddings, people tend to lose their nerve and they embrace the traditional for that "day of days." Grooms and the other males in the wedding party sometimes fall in step quicker than females. The long years of taboos in color and styling have left their mark. Even if the groom does fancy the burgundy velvet jacket with its black moire lapels and collar and its ruffled shirt, he'll often think of the in-laws and rent a par-for-the-occasion plain tux.

The author's prejudice against rentalwear aside, the groom who chooses a more traditional look will probably find it difficult to escape the formalwear-rental industry. Most men are unwilling to put out the substantial amount it would take to buy a formal suit or to have one tailored. (Interesting . . . brides *never* quibble about the price of a good-for-one-day bridal costume.) Even so, if the groom wants to look black tie or white tie, then he's going to have to rent.

If you must rent, the first thing to forget is all the nonsense about what to wear when. Don't drive yourself crazy with seeking the "proper" attire for a formal evening or semiformal evening of whatever season. Consider all that under the boards and discard the helpful little booklets that they pass out to you in the shop for your edification. Remember only that you and the bride should look as if you are both going to be in the same wedding. If the wedding is casual, you both should decide to dress in easy fashion; if it is formal, you both should wear something on the fancy side. You should take seasonal colors and fabrics into consideration only if it pleases you to do so and only if it is mandatory to common sense. You are free to wear dark, or cool-weather, fabrics in summer if you choose and you are just as free to wear white and light fabrics in winter.

Try to rent as individual an outfit as you can manage without surrendering your sense of aesthetics. More of the newer styles are available in a wider assortment than before. Smile, nod, and tune out those determined souls who want to impress on you that nothing but a regulation tux will do. You have choices. If the crushed velvet turns you off, maybe the gray whipcord won't. Manufacturers do seem to be trying to please.

Best and only relief from exploitation in renting clothes is in pricing around. There are differences in price, but you might have to travel to find them. Men's rentalwear shops have been suspected of being old price fixers from away back —especially in urban areas. Better prices are to be found in some suburbs and small towns.

Approximate cost at this writing for a weekend's worth of wear ranges from $18 to about $55 for suit, shirt, and package-deal accessories. The newer styles of jackets, along with flared pants and ruffled shirts, run $28 to $40. The shirts with ruffles, pleats, machine embroidery, or lace are in white and all sherbet colors and rent for $5.00. You can buy the shirt for about $15 to $25.

Some rentalwear shops give the groom a free outfit if his wedding party consists of six or more, including himself. This is now a common come-on. Since the wedding party members pay for their own clothes as a rule, it's a fine way for the groom to get off free. Check around first to make sure the wedding party is not absorbing your expenses by paying prices out of line with other rentalwear establishments. (Of course, you needn't assume that the wedding party must wear formal attire and/or all be dressed alike. If you'd like to avoid having the males in the wedding look as identical as Mao's army, read the last section of this chapter.)

No one is more associated with full dress than dapper Fred

Astaire. He coolly hoofed his way to fortune in formal clothes. Recently a gala was given at the Waldorf Astoria to honor him and Ginger Rogers. Fred showed up in a common dinner suit. Eyebrows raised when at the age of seventy-three Fred Astaire finally let the truth out: He has always hated white tie and tails. He informed a delighted group of reporters that tie and tails are so uncomfortable, he avoids ever wearing them.

God love you Fred Astaire. You speak for men all over the country. But you bring us to a perilous situation. How do you get "dressed up" if you reject the clothes that constitute the recognized state of being "dressed up?"

Here's how: You wear clothes that make you look nice, that are comfortable, and that are feasible for the occasion. At a wedding the occasion is romantic, and all the outlets of romanticism are just as available to the groom. Once you're sold on the abstract of a romantic ideal, the following concrete ideas might help produce your own look.

Wear your own suit. Your newest one—the one that makes you look very *Esquire*. It can be navy, brown, khaki, or striped seersucker. It's yours and it fits you and, to make it right for the occasion, all you need to add is a ruffled shirt. It's amazing what a simple idea this is and how effectively it works. Just try your khaki suit over a brown ruffled shirt and complete it with a bow tie in contrasting warm colors. Or tuck a pale raspberry ruffled shirt under your navy blue suit and top with a navy and white striped bow tie.

There you are—comfortable. You haven't parted with a pocketful of money, the shirt is romantic and festive, and the whole appearance is close enough to propriety to keep the gossipmongers bored.

This outfit is appropriate for any wedding where a rented formal suit of any nature would be appropriate. Don't be convinced otherwise. A few inches added to the tail or cutaway at the waistline do not make the monumental differences in appearance that the wedding biz would want you to believe.

You can rent the shirt ($5.00) or buy it ($15 to $25). Why not buy it? That way it will be all yours and you can trot it out to wear to other people's weddings and fancy occasions, not to mention a sentimental appearance on your own anniversaries.

Another great look for grooms who prefer to wear a jacket is the blazer and white trousers approach. This is a particularly nifty look for summer weddings. A dark navy blazer with white, tailored trousers, a marine blue shirt with tiny, tiny white dots all over, and a white bow tie—dashing, casual, comfortable—will be around for more good times.

For outdoor weddings, sports jackets are just fine. (Madras is on the rebound and if you saved your madras patchwork sports jacket from the early sixties, you were receiving divine inspiration from somewhere.)

Jackets needn't be of the ordinary variety. For a church ceremony, a suit jacket would probably be most comfortable. For an outdoor ceremony, a safari jacket or a hunter's shirt might set just right.

At an early October ceremony on the banks of the Susquehanna River in Pennsylvania, the groom wore a beige safari jacket, with a cream-colored turtleneck underneath it, and deep tan trousers. He also wore a thick wreath of mountain laurel on his head. It really worked.

Indoors or outdoors, there is no law declaring punishment for grooms who don't want to wear jackets. How many August weddings have you attended with the groom and gang in full formal attire ready to bite the aisle runner with heat prostration? It doesn't have to be. Despite parents, bridal consultants, and even the bride's uncertainty, you don't have to wear a jacket. What then?

Well, back to the ruffled or pleated shirt. Wear a ruffled shirt and don't cover it up with a jacket. Accompany it with tailored, well-fitting pants, and other accessories that will make the occasion adequately fancy. Try this on as a groom: a white shirt with ruffles down the front and on the cuffs, black flared knit trousers, a dark red suede belt and a black bow tie with white polka dots. It's a "dressed up" look that makes sense.

For more casual circumstances you could work with any variety of shirts. At a garden wedding a groom wore cream-colored pants and a floral print cotton shirt of soft blues. At a wedding in Albuquerque, New Mexico, the groom wore white trousers, a softly gathered white shirt, and a huge, beautiful belt made of chunks of turquoise and tooled silver.

The loose, gathered shirt has been appearing at weddings. It is known as the Lord Byron or Walt Whitman shirt in some parts of the country and rates 100 per cent on the scale of romanticism. It can be made of any fabric, although it is particularly handsome in pale, thin handwoven cotton. It can be belted, embroidered, or tucked in and looks fantastic when coupled with corduroy pants.

Mexican and Colombian shirts, like Mexican bridal dresses, work well at weddings. Most are raw cotton with tucks and/or colored embroidery. They are particularly adept at outdoor weddings if you are the kind of person who is believable in a peasant look.

Accessories can pull a groom together when nothing else will. If working with traditional formalwear, a bright (perhaps handmade) tie, vest or cummerbund might save the groom from the doldrums. All these garments have served in the past as an outlet for masculine expression in fashion and could easily perform such functions at the celebration of a marriage. They are all relatively easy to buy or make. (Yes, you too could make a bow tie or a vest. There are patterns, fabrics, easy-to-follow directions. You could manage it as easily as the bride. The resulting feelings of achievement and creativity are unrestrained. Fabrics to consider: suede, houndstooth silk, flowered linen, or several red bandanas.)

Belts are an accessory that could add interest to an outfit. Of course if you rent clothes, you're usually stuck with suspenders. With some of the other suggestions above, however, you could wear any belt that struck your fancy and added something to the outfit. You could have a special belt made for the occasion or make one yourself.

Hats are considered accessories, too. Winter hats are a uniform drag. But in summer, a straw skimmer is lighthearted and rather debonaire. At a July wedding in Boston all the ushers as well as the groom showed up in white bucks and skimmers.

Grooms are as much involved in the wedding celebration as brides, although wedding etiquette would have it otherwise. A typical bride goes to any extent, or any expense, to dress for the wedding. She may spend $500 for her dress or fifty days sewing it. The groom rents a suit off a rack. That's how it should be, says the bridal industry.

The Wedding Party

Usually the ushers and bridesmaids wear clothes in tune with the bride and groom. So any of the suggestions that have already appeared for the featured couple will also work well for their friends in the wedding party.

The point to be made here is not what they wear—it's what they *all* wear. Okay, here comes the bride in your average church wedding. And here come the bridesmaids. Five identical pink and lacey dresses, five pink picture hats, five little bouquets of baby's-breath and roses. Of course, the maid of honor has different color ribbons on her bouquet. And yes, their shoes are all dyed to match the dress. God forbid that they should wear different shoes so that a different kind of toe would peak out from under the identical long skirts. These lovely pink girls are boring, plastic, and 99 per cent predictable.

"But it looks so lovely when they're all dressed alike," your mother will say. But why? Is it because the people themselves look lovely or is it because the effort gone into dressing them in a kind of uniform is so touching?

The bridesmaid dresses available for purchase have taken a decided turn for the better. The options for ushers are widening in scope and color. All this individualizing is taking place and yet everyone is determined that the wedding party still must dress exactly alike. Why haven't the ushers and bridesmaids of America protested? I'm not sure. Perhaps it's just because they are a little too polite.

Dare you break all this conformity? That's up to you and the members of your wedding party. You might think about the following guidelines.

First off, the wedding party does take its cue from the attire of the bride and groom. Hopefully, the bride and groom will be dressed in a way that reflects their own personalities and that mode of dress will more or less naturally reflect the personality of their closest friends.

Secondly, everyone should dress as if they're going to the *same wedding. But everyone doesn't have to dress alike.* The idea is to choose clothes that go together, that have the same feeling. The Parlour boutique often sells different styles and different colors of dresses to be worn as bridesmaids' dresses at the same wedding. This usually means two or three dresses with the maximum being four as the trend is away from large wedding parties.

For a country wedding, different calico prints of different colors were handmade by the bridesmaids. The style was the same, made from the same dress pattern, but the variations in the color and design of the fabric were both corresponding and distinguishing. Different style dresses in different floral-print fabrics could go together as well—as long as they have a similar aura about them.

Ushers could wear different-colored, decorated shirts, with ruffles and lace or whatever suited each individual. The thing to avoid is having one usher show up in a blazer, another in a tux, and a third in an ethnic shirt. Not because their choices wouldn't suit each usher, but because the celebration calls for some statement of character.

Finally, decide what makes a statement and what doesn't. Matching shoes or gloves or net-and-doily headpieces provide no clues to the character of the celebration. But perhaps matching bouquets of lilacs would. Or then again, bouquets of different flowers or assorted boutonnieres or whatever would say what should be said of you. Details are just not that important. It's the combination of choices which compose the style of the wedding that is important.

7. THE WEDDING CEREMONY—
A PERSONAL HIGH MOMENT

Five minutes before a wedding ceremony I never know what will happen. I'm fairly certain that it will run decently and in good order. Terrible goofs very seldom happen at weddings. But will it "get off the ground?" Will the couple experience it? You never know. Some of the weddings that you expect to be heartfelt occasions are just spoken words. Others that look like run-of-the-mill weddings are genuine high moments.

VICTOR H. CARPENTER
Minister, Unitarian Universalist Association

An incredible number of married couples have only the dimmest memory of the actual wedding ceremony that cemented their bond. Some have no other memory than having experienced distinct uneasy feelings—the kind of nervous, uncomfortable feelings they have before any audience-attended performance. Most remember the reiterated standards: "for better or for worse, in sickness and in health," "till death do us part," "I do," "You may kiss the bride." But outside of that it's hazy. They feel foolish recalling it. There was a church, a dress, a veil, a wedding cake, they remember all that. That has come to signify their marriage. The happy, plastic decoration that stood on top of the cake is tucked away somewhere. The vows and promises and blessings that stated their marriage are forgotten.

And it's not surprising. I remember watching a very good friend walk down the aisle of a church looking sober and exceedingly nervous. The minister fumbled her name. The vows were barely audible. The groom was stoic but sweating profusely. These were a couple of intelligent, witty people who had a wealth of creative energy. Their prayer-book ceremony was strained and stilted. It didn't fit.

How does a couple make the wedding ceremony a high moment? They do it by making the ceremony their very own. This sounds utterly simplistic, but it is a truth. A wedding service that expresses the most real things that the bride and groom can say to each other is a service that is charged with the true emotions of the relationship. It means something. It matters. It is a beautiful occasion for the couple and for those in attendance.

Start off with the basics. What, first off, is necessary for the completion of a recognized marriage?

Wedding is of Anglo-Saxon derivation coming from the word meaning "to pledge." The pledging involved has only recently involved notions of romantic love. Most marriages were financial transactions—good PR moves. Even this wheeling and dealing was a substantial change from the dark beginnings of weddings. During ancient times no specific marriage rite was required. The ceremony consisted of the sexual consummation itself. There were no vows, no records, no religious or secular officials. Sometimes there were observers at the sexual union, as witnesses. Sometimes there was a party or celebration if the families involved had food to share. If the bride had been stolen—as was sometimes the case—there was only furtiveness and brute force.

In the ancient Judaic traditions only two witnesses were necessary. The presence of a tribal elder wasn't required. If there were no other humans available, Heaven and Earth were considered suitable witnesses.

The early Christian church wanted nothing to do with the dirty business of supporting sexual unions. Weddings within churches were outlawed, but a brother of the church might say a benediction over the couple to ward off the devil as they sped away to consummate the marriage.

What all this points up to is that early weddings were not religious affairs, and they were not legal affairs. They were pairing-off occurrences in monogamous societies calling for a party in good times and nothing but hope in lean times.

All the bureaucracy came about with the rise of the church as a social institution and acquisition of personal wealth that needed to be equitably allotted. The evolution of weddings and marriage that resulted is the sole subject of many cultural tomes.

Today, all that is required in the United States for a legal marriage is that the signature of a clergyman, judge, justice of the peace, mayor, sea captain, or other qualified person, be placed on a validated marriage license. In some, but not all, states, witnesses to the signing of the license are also mandatory. Various requirements are imposed by individual states to obtain a validated marriage license. The blood test and birth certificate are fairly standard as is the waiting period. But legally, there's no more to it than that. (Sign on the dotted line and you're married.)

In fact, the Reverend Cecil Williams of Glide Memorial Methodist Church in San Francisco asks a couple into his office and talks with them about their feelings and plans. If all seems in order at the end of the interview, he nonchalantly informs them that they are now married and, except for civil requirements, they need do no more.

The Reverend Williams is a rare and refreshing clergyman. When the church did become involved in marriage rites, it assumed a dictatorial position that hasn't altered much in over four hundred years. The rules, most of the clergy maintain, are everything. It's tradition that gives the ceremony its value. Men and women in ages past have declared their union this way and, in the eyes of the church, that's how it's got to be done.

Even so, finding a minister who will respect your plans and feelings is less difficult today than it used to be. The turbulence of the sixties gave way to a new outlook, dubbed a new consciousness. Churches and synagogues of the United States picked up a little of this consciousness in an institutional way. Now, most synagogues, Protestant churches, and some Catholic churches are quite willing to incorporate new outlooks into rites of passage common to our culture. In fact, not to do so would mean a continuing demise for these institutions, and most of them know that.

Where to Find a Flexible Officiant

1. If you have a religious background, try your own clergy first. You may be surprised at the minister of your church-school days. There've been ten or twenty years of new ideas that have come his way too. Or maybe the old church or synagogue has been taken over by a new clergyman. Go to him. There's no harm in asking. If you get a lecture and holy words of warning, you can just smile, nod, and leave quickly.

2. Call the local council of churches. Ask for the name of a liberal church complete with liberal minister. They'll know what you mean. In some areas there is even a Council of Liberal Churches. Contact the Union of American Hebrew Congregations for referral to a rabbi of a reformed synagogue. Try the Newman Center or the Catholic Information Center for a priest, although these may not be very helpful. See if you can sniff out a Catholic "underground."

3. Check churches around college campuses. Clergy in these areas usually have flexible ministers who enjoy the new trends in weddings. Or, track down your old college chaplain.

4. Ethical societies and other humanist organizations have meeting places and leaders who are capable of performing weddings but are not clergymen. Most ethical societies are by definition open to the concept of the new wedding.

5. You can usually count on the ministers of the Unitarian-Universalist Association of churches. The UUA ministers respect all religions and creeds. Since they are creedless, they themselves vary in beliefs and degrees of liberality. It seems that UUA ministers specialize in marrying couples who have been alienated from their own churches through divorce, mixed marriage, or just plain disgust. They'll also marry couples who disavow any religious affiliation. Almost all UUA ministers are very contemporary people who not only respect your own plans but can make enlightened suggestions and additions along the lines you have chosen.

Most clergy will marry a couple they don't know. They usually ask for some kind of conference to establish the couple's motives and maturity. (For some UUA clergymen the ratio of strangers to members of the congregation is ten to one.)

If you are not a member of a particular clergyman's congregation, you must realize that he has first obligation to his own membership. Call well in advance to secure a date. Ask about his fee. He will, of course, charge you for his services. Some busy rabbis during the "marrying months" have to perform services for non-members during the week.

Once you've located a clergyman and he has consented to perform your wedding ceremony, he will discuss the ceremony and may pose one of the following approaches:

1. He offers you a sample ceremony—a prototype. He discusses the ceremony with you and assures you that you are free to accept it as is or you may add and subtract to fit your own feelings.

2. He offers you various components of a ceremony for your choice. This is a kind of Chinese menu of vows, readings, benedictions from which you choose one from column A, one from column B, etc.

3. He may ask you to write your own ceremony—from scratch. He may feel that this is the one legitimate way to get your true feelings incorporated into the wedding and he

probably will be willing to help you refine the ceremony if you desire. (This is also a sneaky way to find out if your values, expectations, and goals are in line with each other.)

There are two touchy issues that flare up in dealing with some clergymen. The first is an old issue: MIXED MAR-RIAGE. This is the opposition of a religious organization toward its members marrying "outside their faith." Mixed marriage tends to be a real issue to conservative and orthodox Jews and Catholics. Protestants, it would seem, have given up in resignation long ago except for a few groups of evan-gelicals. Finding a liberal clergymen usually precludes facing a hassle over "mixed marriage." He can provide tactful and knowledgeable assistance if the issue is still a problem with either of your families.

The other issue is "till death do us part." Many members of the clergy will go along with any sincere innovation in a wedding service as long as the participants are playing for keeps. The clergyman may feel very strongly that a vow is understood to be made before God and is therefore a permanent promise. Turning "as long as we both shall live" into "as long as we both shall love" seems to be an obvious escape clause to clergymen—a weakening of society's basic family unit. To others, it's indicative of a lack of commit-ment.

If you feel that the honesty of your pledges requires the abolishment of the "forever" concept, you must air your feel-ings with the officiant early in your talks. This is an issue that shouldn't be left to misunderstanding late in the game.

Clergymen tend to be thought of as the prime officiants at wedding ceremonies because they hold the key to the church door and for so many years weddings in churches were con-sidered "de rigueur." If your wedding is to be held outside a church and is to be a secular rather than a religious ceremony, you might want to contact a justice of the peace. The J.P. can offer you two advantages. 1. He will travel to the chosen site of your ceremony. He doesn't mind if it is outdoors, in your home, or out in the alley. If it's within reasonable distance of his establishment, he'll be there. 2. The Justice has his own ceremonies which you can choose from. But the big advantage is that he will read any ceremony you write. He has no axes to grind or crosses to bear about what you choose to say at your wedding service.

The old J.P. in his little living-room office is a thing of the past in many states. Now these civil officials are connected with district courts. Still, the old image persists—the midnight Justice of the Peace in rumpled pjs marrying a scared young couple while his kind wife holds the Bible. That's Currier & Ives stuff now. You must contact the "Squire"— as they are addressed—and arrange a date in advance. Take the ceremony (carefully typed, double spaced) to him beforehand and explain all procedures. He will discuss his fee which is from $20 for marriage in his office to $50 for a house call. (Most area "house calls" are around $30 to $40.) Justices of the Peace are listed in the yellow pages of your phone directory.

Despite the flexibility of J.P.s, they are usually a less personal officiant than is a clergyman. Most clergymen want to know more about you than your name and the results of your blood test. The clergy is more sensitive to the spirit of marriage. But while an officiant of the cloth is more spiritual and sensitive, a Justice of the Peace is often more practical.

Judges are usually the officiants in civil ceremonies. They are the poorest officiants of all. Unless you know a judge personally and he is willing to read your personalized service, you will be "next" in the procession of those waiting for the judge "on wedding duty." Judges have a set service that they read. They are suspicious of innovations. The best they can be is "kindly." As for locale, City Hall weddings—especially in large cities—are the epitome of sterility.

Whether you choose someone from the religious sector or

someone from the civil sector, the officiant at your wedding is what his title implies—an officiant. He himself does not have the power to form a union between the two of you. Only you have that power. You have already made the bond with your stated intention to marry; your decision has married you. The officiant and guests are there to recognize that you are husband and wife.

It often seems that officiants help themselves to the status of being author of the marriage. ("I now pronounce you man and wife.") This is incorrect wording and should be reconsidered in the writing of an original ceremony. A subtle point, but an important one. Self-declared marriage is part of the attitude that is responsible for the wedding-ceremony "high."

I, —————————, take thee, —————————, to my
wedded Wife, to have and to hold from this day
forward, for better for worse, for richer for poorer,
in sickness and in health, to love and to cherish,
till death we do part, according to God's holy
ordinance; and thereto I plight thee my troth.

The Book of Common Prayer, 1789

I, —————————, take you, —————————, to be
my wife (husband), and these things I promise you:
I will be faithful to you and honest with you;
I will respect, trust, help and care for you;
I will share my life with you;
I will forgive you as we have been forgiven;
and I will try with you better to understand our-
selves, the world and God;
Through the best and the worst of what is to come
as long as we live.

Suggested Lutheran marriage vow, 1972

I will be your husband, Elizabeth. I give you all my

love without reservation. We have so many joyful times ahead of us—many decisions and many possibilities. I promise to place our personal growth and the continuous growth of our love above all other considerations. I will be honest with you. I will accept you as an equal and unique individual. I will be open with my affection and support. Together I know that we can build a life filled with satisfactions. I'm so happy we found each other. I love you.

Marriage service of Peter Loring
and Elizabeth Mussmanto

Wording the Wedding

The above three vows seem to represent the categories of wordings you might choose. The first is wholly traditional. The second is a revised version of the traditional vow as suggested by the Lutheran Church of America. The third is from the heart and head of a twenty-six-year-old man named Peter Loring.

The first change in many decades of wedding service sameness dawned in the fifties. It then became a trend for the couple to memorize and recite their own vows rather than repeating the vows phrase by phrase as uttered by the officiant. This met with no resistance. Everyone thought it was a fine idea that the couple show sufficient ambitiousness to go to the trouble of committing the vows to memory. It was a widely accepted practice and the earmark of your "educated" young couple.

That this step should follow the social upheavals of World War II is no surprise. It's significant in that it was the first move in putting the act of marrying into the hands of those being married. More and more clergymen were realizing the disparity in the importance of the wedding ceremony and the importance of the language that comprised that ceremony.

The vows just weren't saying anything. (The divorce rate was climbing, too.) It gave one pause.

Recently, an Episcopal minister noted how absurd he had come to view his practice of talking over the marriage service with the couple in prewedding conferences, explaining phrases like "I plight thee my troth."

"What does that mean to a twenty-three-year-old man or woman—'I plight thee my troth'?" he lamented. "Absolutely nothing."

To some young couples it does have significance. It means generations of forebears citing the same oaths. It means continuity; it means form and assurance. All clergy have on hand at least two varieties of a wedding service that are marked by their bonds to tradition. For traditionalists, there's no problem.

Even within the traditional wording, personalization has become a common practice. The suggested Lutheran vow is open to almost any change that the couple finds meaningful. (Its one stipulation is that the "as long as we live" sentiment stays.) This vow and others like it are fast becoming the accepted type of wedding language. It eliminates Old English; it acknowledges current values as well as timeless standards. It is a statement of sharing that rings true to the ear. If as a couple you find its religious and permanency connotations within your concept of marriage, then it might fit your needs.

The third vow comes out of the enormity of the blank page and the full mind. It is the most difficult to choose because it starts without benefit of format and it usually becomes a studied work of perfection—rewritten and revised. It eloquently states the specific marriage promises that Peter Loring is making to Elizabeth Mussmanto. It is completely their own, strengthened by plucking out wordings from here and there, reworking them, sifting out the unimportant, and accurately stating the important principles. The whole wedding service was compiled in the same manner. Every aspect was distinctly Peter and Elizabeth, from the introduction through the music and readings and finally the close, a poem read by Peter's best friend.

In the context of this discussion, there are only two rather obvious ground rules for the writing of original vows. They are:

1. The contents must be a sincere expression of the couple's feelings for each other.
2. The vow must be worthy of the occasion.

One liberal minister who has officiated at many personalized weddings had to veto the vows of a couple who write such pettiness as ". . . and never to criticize her hairdos." And ". . . never to serve him frozen foods." This kind of detail is way out of place in a wedding vow. It may be more in line for a marriage contract. (More about contracts later.)

Vows need not be identical. (Traditionally, an identical vow is repeated by both partners with perhaps an extra "obey" clause thrown in for the woman's part.) Original vows could hardly be expected to be identical. If you are taking a standard or updated vow and adding your own touches to it, try to make the changes separately without consulting each other. The vow each of you comes up with is the one each of you should use as your promise.

In the sixties, politics infiltrated the wedding vows of America's involved youth. Since those with political motivations seemed to be the ones trying new things, it was no accident that the early "new" weddings included vows of nonviolence, concern for poverty, and hopes for ecology and racial equality. Research for this book indicates that there are very few altruistic or political vows being uttered in the seventies. Perhaps people have all stepped back into their own lives, especially those who are absorbed with the tremendously involving task of joining their lives.

If there is some human concern that represents an important part of your hopes for the future, you can feel free to express it at a time when you are stating terms and ideas and emotions. This should be a concern shared by both of you. It would be best stated clearly and briefly to avoid a feeling of soapboxing at the ceremony.

If this subject is sure to cause commotion, consider why it is you want it brought up at your wedding. A Harvard and a Radcliffe graduate, who both joined the Jesus movement, were married in a ceremony to which their Jewish and agnostic parents were invited. At one point in the ceremony the couple faced the audience and proceeded to tell just what it was that "Jesus has done for me." The ceremony promptly turned into a wake, with both sets of parents weeping through the rest of the day. The couple's intentions had been to convince their parents of their newfound happiness and to hopefully cause their parents to consider the merits of salvation. What they said was sincere and relevant to their present lives. But to the parents it was cruelly alien on their children's wedding day. It was an obvious source of contention. The same ideas could have been voiced at a less emotional time that would have allowed far more understanding to take place. Wedding-day moral: Don't preach; don't proselytize; don't alienate. Despite the above don'ts, it is easy to find a way to state what is important to you. Through readings or wordings within the ceremony, you can make clear your hopes and concerns without turning them into mountainous issues.

It seems there are several "old" ideas which were always a part of traditional ceremonies that are still finding their way into contemporary weddings through accident, or usually through thoughtlessness. The objections voiced to these ideas are my own. I raise them in deference to the psychological freedom of men and women. You may agree with these editorializings or you may disagree, but please consider the following:

1. The mention of offspring should be eliminated from the wedding ceremony in wording and in prayer. Marriage is a bonding of two adults. Children via marriage used to be society's only sane means of survival, and religious and cultural institutions pushed hard for offspring. This is no longer the necessity it used to be. A couple just forming their own bond needs to be given a chance to decide about children once they've become familiar with the course of their own relationship. Most will decide to have children; some will decide against having them. It's the expectation that all newly married couples are parents-to-be that must be eliminated.

2. The "one flesh" clause should be scratched. "One flesh" was, of course, a euphonism for sexual intercourse. It grew to mean more than that, though. It was the "one flesh" idea that lost a woman her identity through the bond of marriage. (If there were only one flesh, it was his.) Marriage is the coming together of two equal units to form a loving partnership. Even in the act of intercourse we are not "one flesh." Most people who like themselves don't want to be one flesh; they hope to offer their own particular love to another distinct individual who is deserving of that love.

3. At the end of the ceremony the officiant pronounces you man and wife. The term man and wife is an obvious term of possession. Man and his wife. They are not equal labels. The man is still a man but the woman has become a wife. If man is to woman as husband is to wife, then the status of a pair of newlyweds is husband and wife.

4. Furthermore, it's questionable whether the officiant has the power to make this proclamation at all. He can ask that the congregation hereafter recognize the couple as husband and wife, he can say that the couple has pronounced themselves husband and wife, he can acknowledge their new status as husband and wife, but he really can't pronounce them husband and wife. That is a pronunciation that only the couple can make.

5. Wedding vows are enormously personal rites. They are addressed to each other, FACING EACH OTHER, not facing the officiant. If there is a part of the vow that is personal, it could be uttered in a soft voice not intended for the audience's ears —a secret vow.

One couple, married in 1969, believed that the occasion of their marriage was so special and sacred that no words would suffice. The ceremony consisted of the couple walking around the interior of a huge old church—up one aisle and down the other. When they reached the altar, the minister announced that they had pronounced themselves husband and wife.

Ceremonial Signings

Nobody is yet quite sure about the true role of a marriage contract. The marriage contracts attempted to date-define and outline agreements on subjects such as finances, child-rearing, in-law relations, and careers, as well as provisions for separation. Even supporters of a mutually drawn marriage contract agree that it is experimental, unenforceable and may be, at best, a good way for the couple to line up their mutual interests and life styles for a prewedding comparison. Since a contract is a specific agreement between two people about the understandings and expectations pertaining to their marriage, it certainly could have a place in the wedding ceremony itself. If a contract is to be drawn up, it should be done well in advance (certainly in advance of the wedding plans) and signed in its final form at the ceremony. This signing might lend the contract a kind of authority that the laws of the land have not yet agreed to grant it. As of now, you can't sue for divorce on grounds of breech of contract.

If the idea of a contract filled with specifics makes you edgy, you might consider drawing up a general statement of purpose to be signed at the wedding ceremony. This statement could contain just about any hope, sentiment, or principle that you have found to be worthy of carrying into the more permanent state of marriage. If such a statement of purpose is short and worthy of the occasion, it could be read aloud as part of the ceremony. A contract, by its specific nature, probably wouldn't lend itself to a reading.

The signing of documents at a marriage is nothing new. Most couples must sign a certificate of marriage or the church register on their wedding day and witnesses must sign too. Usually this takes place after the ceremony.

At orthodox and conservative Jewish ceremonies the ketubah, a certificate of marriage signed by the rabbi and two witnesses, is presented to the couple but not read at the ceremony. In the past the ketubah was often a work of art, commissioned by the family and carefully hand designed with illustration and fine calligraphy. If a statement of purpose is to be read and/or signed at the wedding, perhaps the statement itself could be lettered and illustrated by one of the couple's talented friends or even a professional artist. Whether framed for display or tucked away, it seems a far more important memento than a plastic cake decoration.

One of the most distinctive signings takes place in the traditional Quaker wedding service. The signing of the marriage certificate marks the end of a wedding service held in the quiet manner of the Friends. A signing table is placed at the front of the Meeting House and the certificate itself is presented to the couple by a chosen friend or member of the family.

Choreography

Many are the wedding books that will tell you the correct order of the wedding procession, how the attendants are to walk and who is going to stand where. If the wedding books don't get you, the director of the rehearsal does, whether it's the officiant or the "parish wedding hostess." Granted, some order must abound. It would seem in good form for the wedding party to have a feeling for the logistics of what is about to happen. However, most weddings are rather unimaginative about the choreography of parties advancing or recessing from here to there.

What usually happens is that the ushers, then the bridesmaids two-step it up the aisle and the LOVELY BRIDE follows. Meanwhile, waiting in full view at the altar are the groom, the best man, and the officiant. (Two out of three of those at the altar are probably not enjoying being displayed motionless before a crowd.)

The bride, marching altarward on the arm of her proud father, is being figuratively given from one male to another. "Who gives this woman to be married to this man?" No one cares who is giving the man. It's assumed that he is a free person; no one would presume to give him away.

Although most of today's women are on to the meaning of the giving-away detail, many of them find it "so hard to disappoint Dad." As one bride put it, "Mom was always talking about the dress and the occasion, but only twice during my childhood did my father mention giving me away at a wedding ceremony. Both times were very serious moments. It was more than just a formality to him."

There is a compromise solution to this dilemma—one that works well and appeases most fathers. The father of the bride can indeed escort his daughter down the aisle. When they reach the first or second pew, where the mother of the bride is sitting, the father kisses his daughter and takes a seat by his wife. The daughter walks to the altar herself to meet the groom. The "who gives this woman" wording is cut from the ceremony.

The reason that the choreography of traditional weddings is so fixed is that the choreography itself is a part of the ceremony. It says something. It is the ordering of the participants and their presentation. If the march down the aisle, starring the bride and her father, doesn't suit the feeling of your wedding, there are alternatives. These suggestions, of course, may not fit your wedding either, in which case the choreography that you decide upon is undisputedly the most appropriate.

In a situation that calls for a processional, the bride and groom can walk up the aisle hand in hand. There is no canon law that makes this impossible. Its significance is important —the two of you are entering into marriage together, fully aware of yourselves and each other. In this country veiled brides don't meet parentally chosen grooms at the altar for the first time. Why should the bride be led up the aisle ceremoniously to meet the groom? If it is true that the couple are pronouncing their own marriage, then it is fitting for them to ascend to the altar as coconspirators.

If the wedding takes place in a two-aisle church or auditorium, perhaps the groom could proceed to the altar in one of the aisles and the bride could simultaneously come up the other aisle. This would make an equalitarian approach to the joining ceremony at the altar.

In traditional Jewish ceremonies the procession includes all the family principals: the grandparents of the bride, the grandparents of the groom, bridesmaids and ushers, followed by the groom, flanked by his parents, and the bride by hers. This means that in traditional Jewish ceremonies the groom as well as the bride is given away and by both parents, not just the father. There's lots to be said for this kind of processional. First of all, it's an eloquent proclamation of family unity and continuum. If the bride and groom have a "sense of family," strong family ties and backing, this kind of processional marks a joyful occasion for everyone. There is no reason that it should be restricted to Jewish ceremonies. If this kind of feeling fits your wedding, you could make many people (including yourselves) proud and happy.

At a wedding in a chapel, private home, or reception room, the bride and groom could be at the entrance together to greet guests as they enter. This is a warm, friendly gesture and would almost preclude any kind of processional. In fact, if the bride and groom have been living together for some time, it would seem particularly right and natural.

Outdoor weddings leave way for manifold alternatives in choreography. The unexpected seems to be more common than the traditional. Just one example: Following the old Elizabethan custom, the bride in a 1973 wedding was escorted to the place of marriage in the midst of her female friends and the groom was ushered in by a cluster of his friends. Adding a new gesture, all the friends joined hands in a circle around the bride, groom, and officiant for the saying of the vows.

No matter how the choreography is arranged for the entrance to the ceremony, the members of the bridal party walk naturally, avoiding the two-step used for ceremonial occasions. The static, "step-to-the-beat" mentality of the two-step only makes the guests aware that the group probably "practiced." It's demonstrative, uncomfortable, and serves no noble purpose. Nervous bridesmaids in high-heeled shoes sway visably when they're two-stepping to slow music, and two-stepping ushers take themselves much too seriously.

Once the tumultuous journey to the altar has ended—what then?

One of the aspects about the present wedding system that many clergy would like to change is the lack of participatory feeling on the part of the guests. There they are, sitting in pews, watching the backs of the bride and groom. Perhaps the bride's trip down the aisle has such neck-craning importance for them because they can't see or hear anything once the actual ceremony gets underway. They are cut off.

When the wedding guests number under thirty, Victor Carpenter, a Unitarian Universalist minister, asks them to leave their seats and stand around the bride and groom at the front of the church. In churches and other restricted areas, thirty guests are about all that could participate in this spontaneous inclusion. Outdoors, all the guests might easily surround the couple, no matter what their number.

Whether this plan is operable or not, the single biggest choreographic point at the altar is the position of the bride and groom. They should be facing each other, not the officiant. This is really important. Their vows and all their attention are addressed to each other. They are after all facing each other to get married. Logistically, this facing serves to include the guests in their rightful roles as witnesses as well as including the officiant in his role as chief witness. In facing each other they have made each other the sole recipient of the magic of the moment and they have allowed their friends and family to observe the public expression of their love.

If there is no recessional, everyone kisses, shakes hands, and hugs on the spot. If there is a recessional, it is usually a joyful affair, the music is faster, brighter, the members of the wedding seem to whisk out of the church.

In the recessional it is common to have each usher take the arm of a bridesmaid and have them leave the church as couples behind the bride and groom. While this is an efficient system for clearing out the church, it doesn't symbolize the event that has just occurred. There is only one couple being formed—the bride and groom. They leave as a pair and none of the other parties have a right to mimic that pair. The ushers and bridesmaids can follow out the bride and groom singly as they did when entering or as a group if that's how they entered.

Music

A wedding without music?

The joy of music belongs at everyone's wedding! Music can uniquely express your feelings and set the mood of the day. Discovering the right kind of music takes some consideration and perhaps some research. The results are exciting.

If your wedding is in a church, there may be an organist or pianist who will play. For such services you usually pay a fee similar to that of the clergyman. In some churches it is obligatory to use that church's musical director, as he or she is often called. Talk to the musical director and see what is offered. Explain the tone of your wedding and ask for suggestions. The musical director should have a large repertoire of selections to offer. If not, consider obtaining other musical talent and/or keeping the musical director solely for a specific use, i.e., playing the processional on the organ.

In small churches the clergyman often comes up with musical suggestions. In fact, clergymen may themselves have a musical bent. In not so small Sacred Heart Cathedral in Rochester, New York, Rev. Lawrence Gross has been known to play the guitar and sing some of the religious folk music being requested by young couples for their weddings. When the music is over, he puts down the guitar and officiates at the ceremony.

If you're not sure that you like or understand what the church is offering or if there is no source of musical knowledge at the place where you're being married, seek the advice of experts. They aren't particularly hard to find. Start with a record store—one that specializes in "classical" music. The proprietors and salespeople in these stores are usually a storehouse of musical data. If you explain what you want to a sympathetic ear, you will probably get more suggestions than you can handle. By starting with classical music you'll be able to determine whether you want all, some, or none of the music at your wedding to be classical.

If you opt for contemporary music, you can enter just about any record shop and put the sales personnel through the same paces. (Somewhere along this road paved with free advice, you'll probably feel obliged to buy a record.)

There are lists of music suitable for weddings—both classical and contemporary selections. Three of the four reference books suggested at the end of this chapter contain such a list. (*The Celebration of Marriage* is the only one that does not.) With a list in hand it might be easier to approach both musical director and record shop.

If you're still confused and uncertain and nothing seems to ring quite right, you'll need more direct help. Try the old ask-around survey. Ask around for someone who knows someone who has a degree of knowledge about the subject. This may or may not turn up an authority.

Put a note on the student bulletin board of the nearest college of music or music department within the nearest university. Offer a sum of money (say, $25) for a musical consultant to just advise you on obtaining music for your wedding. Make sure that the note implies consulting work only. Fees for performing are much higher. If this doesn't attract any attention, you might set up an appointment with one of the instructors in the school.

The local library, if it is large, will have a music section or an entire music department with listening devices. The librarian here may be another source of expertise. Music schools and universities have very complete musical libraries as well.

All this is supposing that you have very little musical knowledge or preferences. Most young people know what kind of music they like and are only afraid that contemporary music isn't suitable for weddings. Not so.

Consider selections by Bob Dylan, Judy Collins, The Moody Blues, Simon and Garfunkel, John Denver, Cat Stevens, Richie Havens, Jacques Brel, Joan Baez, Roberta Flack, James Taylor, and Loggins and Massino. All of these performers have albums which contain a song or two that would capture the feeling of love that you want to express.

Folksy groups like Peter, Paul and Mary, or the Seekers,

have cut great romantic pieces on their albums. Popular songs such as "We've Only Just Begun" or "For All We Know" are sung by various artists; sheet music is available if you have your own artist in mind.

Bach, particularly as played on the electronic synthesizer, the soft piano compositions of Eric Satie, or the romances of Debussy would all work well at a wedding. Musicals appeal to some people. Popular singers and new songs are released weekly. There will be appropriate music of the day no matter when you marry.

And certainly not least of all is the hymn. Old-fashioned hymns are being rediscovered for the fine folk music that they are. Since many have religious themes and marvelous melodies, they might fit a certain type of wedding well. ("Amazing Grace" has been the most popularized; there are many others equally as fine.)

But what's all this talk of records, you ask? There is no reason that you shouldn't have recorded music at your wedding if you have a good sound system and someone to handle it. Probably the best solution is to tape what music you want, attach it to adequate-sized speakers, and ask a friend to hit the play button on cue.

If you feel that you'd prefer live music, you've opened up another field of choices. At recent weddings the following combinations have performed: a recorder group playing medieval airs, a cello choir playing in a museum-gallery wedding, two guitars and a flute doing Scottish ballads, a group of french horns playing "Greensleeves," flute solos from Debussy, a combo of two guitars, and a violin playing country music.

In a church service wedding in Ohio, the sister of the bride danced to music from *Missa Luba*. Another friend sang Renaissance airs and another played a flute selection.

It's great to have friends who are talented enough to provide music for your wedding. Using the talents of your friends is in the spirit of the new wedding. There are loads of possibilities and only two pitfalls to watch for.

First pitfall: Make sure that your friends are endowed with a fair amount of talent and performing ability. A sister of the bride wanted to play the wedding march on the huge pipe organ at her sister's wedding. She wasn't a great player to begin with and had only limited experience with an organ and no experience with a giant pipe organ. Every week she had the musical director running to the church to help her learn. She was really in over her head, but everyone had it set in their mind that she would be the one to play her sister's wedding march. On the wedding day she performed dismally. Family and guests ended up feeling embarrassed for her.

Second pitfall: Don't let the music run away with the wedding. Music can add and subtract. One wedding between two students of the Curtis School of Music was backed by music so splendid that it overshadowed everything about the ceremony. As a wedding present, friends of the couple formed a thirteen-piece brass choir that was accompanied by the church's huge choir organ. The music was dramatic and perfectly executed. But it upstaged everything. It sounded like a coronation, like a solid wall of sound. Once the bride was up the aisle and the music stopped, the show was over.

Readings

Readings, poems, and selected prayers for use at the ceremony seem to be a more personal matter than music. There is such a plethora of material to choose from.

It seems that the reading on marriage from *The Prophet* by Kahlil Gibran has been read and reread at personalized weddings. Its sentiments are lovely, but it has become almost expected fare and therefore trite. Perhaps one of the reasons it is read so often is that it deals specifically with the relation-

ship of marriage. You needn't feel that you have to be quite
so literal.

The best sources of material are authors and books that
are your own favorites. Although the reading should be appropriate to the mood of the occasion, it doesn't have to be
about marriage, love, or religion. It could convey some of
your feelings about life, people, or celebrations.

Consider readings from the following:

The poems of Carl Sandburg, Marianne Moore, Robert
Frost, John Ciardi, Edna St. Vincent Millay, Rainer Maria
Rilke.

The classic poets: William Shakespeare, Walt Whitman,
Elizabeth Barrett Browning.

Lyrics to songs that have been particularly important to
both of you.

American Indian poetry—simple and expressive.

Thoughts from the prose of Pierre Teilhard de Chardin,
Erich Fromm, Rollo May, Herman Hesse, or Dag Hammar-
skjold.

The Velveteen Rabbit by Margery Williams (Doubleday)
is a children's story with a beautiful passage about being
loved and growing old.

Hymns for the Celebration of Life, (The Beacon Press)

This is a Unitarian Universalist Association hymnal with
readings in the back. It has a liberal, life-conscious slant. (I
think that reading 402 is particularly good.)

If you have chosen scriptural readings, try to find a
Phillips' translation of the New Testament, or a modern
interpretation of the Psalms.

Choose the work of any contemporary poet, novelist, or
journalist that speaks what you know to be true and worth
reading on the occasion of your marriage.

The object is to find a reading that expresses with beauty
and candor both the obvious and the less obvious nuances
in your relationship and your life. The readings can be time-

less or contemporary. What they show is a humanist spirit in general and a loving spirit in particular.

When it comes to writing a wedding service, there is actually an embarrassment of riches to contend with. There are so many sources to draw from, so many formats, symbolisms, arrangements. Many beautiful words have already been written that could best express your own feelings. Even if you are not going to write a word of your service, you still will have a time trying to collect and edit it; there is much to choose from. For those who are serious about composing a ceremony, there are three fine books available today that give careful consideration to all the options. They are about the wedding service and nothing else—sample ceremonies, vows, benedictions, readings, music. Any one of them would contain enough material to help you put together a personalized service. They are the following:

Khoren Arisian, *The New Wedding: Creating Your Own Marriage Ceremony*. New York: Random House, Inc., 1973.

Vincent B. Silliman, William J. Robbins, Robert C. Sallies, *The Celebration of Marriage*. Norway, Maine: Oxford Hills Press, 1972. (A publication of the Northeast District of the Unitarian Universalist Association, 10 Congress Square, Portland, Maine 04101.)

Brill Halpin and Genné, *Write Your Own Wedding*, New York: Association Press, 1973.

8. FLOWERS AND OTHER
BEAUTIFUL IDEAS

Flowers "dress up" a wedding. Besides their decorative function as festive objects of color and beauty, they lend an important symbolism. They are nature's representatives of "new life." Couples may change or eliminate items from their wedding, but flowers usually prevail.

And so do "wedding flowers." Flowers for weddings usually take the form of a white bouquet for the bride, matching floral bouquets for the bridesmaids, matching boutonnieres for the ushers, corsages for mothers, altar arrangements, and reception centerpieces. As a rule, all these arrangements, except the bride's white bouquet, are color co-ordinated to the bridesmaids' dresses. Ask any florist and he'll tell you—the bridesmaids' dresses are the foundation.

This probably happens because many brides don't have a better idea. They visit their florist, he or she asks them what colors they want, what kind of flowers they want, what their budget limitations are, and they fall in step with the commonplace. According to some florists there have been brides who don't even care: "I don't know anything about flowers. Arrange something pretty for me." Or mothers of the bride who take over flower duty.

It really is too bad. Because the florist is one bridal supplier who, depending on season and money, can do just about anything you want. And many florists are willing.

If you want to stay with white, there are lots of white flowers to work with. The usual choices are roses, daisies, orchids, gardenias, carnations, and chrysanthemums, with a spray of stephanotis or orange blossoms thrown in for good measure. Even though the flowers themselves are beautiful, the result of an all-white bouquet is neither festive nor romantic. Perhaps it's just that everyone is expecting a white bouquet. Perhaps white flowers against a white dress were never supposed to look any other way than "pure."

There are so many wonderful, colorful choices. If your wedding is in the period between December through April, you have all the bulb flowers to choose from. The greenhouses of America are filled with forced blossoms of iris, narcissus, daffodils, tulips, anemones, and some lilies. Freesia, a colorful and fragrant beauty, is often overlooked during this period. In December you can gather the Christmas feeling with poinsettias, Christmas roses, holly, ivy, and even Christmas cactus blooms. Toward April the hyacinth, violet, and lily are for sale in even the most primitive of flower shops. Soon back yards will be filled with lilacs.

Oddly enough, the worst month for flowers is June—the traditional month of weddings. By June the greenhouses have just about burned themselves out and the outdoor selections are yet to come. However, flowers that are still being imported from flower farms in California and Florida are available year round—carnations, roses, orchids, gardenias, daisies, and chrysanthemums. Also, in May and early June the full-blown peony makes its short-lived appearance and lilies of the valley are in stock.

Summer brings all the beautiful garden flowers: larkspur, zinnias, candytuft, buddleia, marigolds, tritonia, snapdragon, and geraniums. (Bright red geraniums make a *gorgeous* bouquet arranged with assorted greens and sprigs of small white, blue, and/or yellow accent flowers. Pink geraniums have a special charm, too.)

In the late summer and fall the vast varieties of chrysanthemums and crepe myrtles are ready for use. And then the greenhouse cycle starts up again.

All this—and the bride carries nondescript white flowers. Well, some brides are breaking the white barrier. There are those who have ventured to pale pink roses mixed with daisies and there are those who have refused to compromise on color.

One June bride carried a loose round bouquet of bright orange, mid-century lilies, fluffy white sprigs of candytuft and pink roses, all accented with the smooth green of *Hosta* leaves.

A February bride held bright red and blue anemones surrounded by delicate fronds of fern.

In March a bouquet of gay yellow freesia was combined with small, blue oriental iris and white violets.

A May bride carried a basket with large heads of deep purple iris, surrounded by the faintest pink puff of peonies, and leafy branches from a weeping tree.

It goes on and on. Even given your flower shop standards —roses, carnations, etc.—you can come up with a happy combination that expresses your own tastes and personalities. Your bouquet need have nothing to do with those the bridesmaids carry. Their flowers don't have to match yours and they can be designed so they needn't clash.

Along with the choice of flowers goes the choice of how to wear or carry them. Today florists have what they call loose rounds, tight colonial nosegay formations, weeping or trailing cascade arrangements, and the "Miss America" arm-styling arrangements. Each lends itself to certain types of flowers and tastes. Florists also decorate baskets, muffs, fans, parasols, and any other accessory that will bear flowers. A well-known florist told of arranging flowers on white oriental fans for a wedding in the city's Chinatown district.

Flowers for the hair—usually in the form of a garland or attached to a headpiece—are becoming more popular. A florist in a very small town said that he had made daisy garlands for the heads of all members of the wedding party, male and female. The wedding took place in a grassy meadow that was part of a state park.

Many brides want to escape the structured look of floral arrangements. They would rather have a more natural look—often a look of more abundance. The bride who carries an armful of freshly cut lilacs or a handful of blue cornflowers and marigolds has established a more informal feeling. (This is called the "European" look by florists. In Europe it is common for the bride to carry a sheath of roses or other flowers, unarranged except possibly for a ribbon tying the stems together.)

Flowers for the bridesmaids add a festive air, but they needn't be a tight match with their dresses and the bouquets don't have to be identical. It might be interesting to have one bridesmaid carry a daffodil bouquet, one a bright tulip arrangement, one a group of lilies, etc.

The same variation goes for flowers for the male members of the wedding. Usually flowers for males are limited to boutonnieres due to male "traditions." They needn't be. In Elizabethan times the groom was adorned by his men with rosettes and ribbon streamers in colors chosen by the bride. Find out how the men in the wedding party feel about flowers.

A common awareness-sensitivity exercise is to ask a group of people what kind of flower each of them feels like. The answers are often accurate reflections of personality, physical characteristics, and individual tastes. Maybe the members of your wedding party can make some very "on target" choices of their own.

Blooming Costs

The cost and amount of flowers needed for decorating the wedding's participants are sometimes minuscule compared to the cost and elaborateness of floral decorations for the site of the ceremony or reception. Church and reception decorations are where the florist makes big bucks. If you are so inclined, you can get the florist's bill up to five or six thousand dollars by decorating with wedding canopies and by ordering arrangements for church window sills, reception tables, and elaborate altarpieces. You could also go for pew bouquets, candelabra decorations, aisle ribbons, bows and runners, and a special throw-away bouquet.

A florist of a long-established firm told (with reserved glee) of a marriage held on the first hole of a golf course. A canopy, beribboned and laden with white flowers, waited at the end of a flowered path winding up the green. When arranging the wedding, the mother of the bride had walked the florist through the adjoining country club where the reception was to be held and ordered arrangements of color-co-ordinated flowers for all "unseemly" corners of the lobby, powder room, dining area, etc.

Probably you don't want to construct the flowered gateway to heaven but you do want to decorate yourselves and possibly the area in which the ceremony is to be held. How do you obtain the effect you want and how do you limit cost? There are two approaches. You can work through a florist or you can act as your own florist. Also, these two options can be combined in any number of ways.

Using a florist needn't be terribly expensive nor need it result in commonplace wedding arrangements. Find a florist who has a large, fresh selection of flowers. Of course, there are price differences between florists. However, since most florists import standards like roses and carnations from warmer climates, their resale costs are fairly similar.

Larger shops that run their own gardens and greenhouses will have a larger selection of less common flowers than those which depend entirely on flower wholesalers.

Go to the florist together and spend lots of time holding groupings of flowers to get the right visual combinations. (If the florist won't let you do this, you're in the wrong store.) Taking flowers out of the refrigerated case and holding them together in your hand will give you a fair idea of the kind of arrangement that will result. Ask to see greens that could surround the flowers, too. For some reason, samples of the greens used are seldom kept in stock. Ask if there will be additional flowers available by the date of your wedding. Ask the price of everything. If nothing appeals to you, go home and think about it some more or go to another florist.

Florists charge for labor and materials. If you buy the flowers and arrange them yourself, you have cut a big chunk from the florist bill. You might want to order the bouquets or garlands already arranged, while ordering cut flowers to arrange yourself as decorations for ceremony site and reception.

Palms and large ferns that stand altarside are rented from the florist. They come with stands and often with lighting fixtures to shine a soft glow up through the green. They vary tremendously in cost. For instance, the range of rented green runs from $75 for three cybodium ferns on underlit pedestals to $10 for one good-sized palm. If you're going to rent large plants, you should price around.

Florists have package wedding plans including all the arrangements ordinarily used in weddings. The prices of the plans are dependent on which flowers are used. A chrysanthemum wedding can be had for $60, a carnation wedding for $100, a rose wedding for $150, a gardenia wedding for $200, and an orchid wedding for $250. Since florists prices have jumped 25 per cent in the past two years, these figures will soon be history. They are presented as a guide to the hierarchy of floral expense. The package deals, which include such niceties as a white aisle runner, are the prototypes of wedding flowers. Very little room for individualization allowed. However, the cost is considerably lower than "à la carte."

The advantage of dealing with a florist is that he takes care of getting the flowers to the church on time, setting up anything that needs setting up, and making sure the flowers are correct and "nicely" arranged.

If you choose to side-step the florist, you can create adequate and relatively cheap floral coverage on your own. This is especially true if you're being married at a time of the year when the world around you is in bloom—when there are free flowers. Here are some suggestions based on ideas carried out in recent weddings.

At a wedding in July, the wedding party collected all kinds and colors of flowers from the gardens of friends and family on the morning of the wedding. For bouquets, the flowers were arranged in bunches and tied with ribbons and trails of miniature ivy. The remaining flowers were placed all over the church in green glass containers. The containers were cut from green wine bottles by the bride's younger brother, who used an inexpensive glass cutter for the project. Corsages for the mothers of the bride and groom were also made by hand. The altar of the church was filled with garden flowers, set in their containers on various platforms to produce a graduated height effect. Ivy was added as greenery.

At a wedding held on a patio in mid-May, boxes of annuals, sold at the local nursery, were wrapped in white tissue paper and used to line the outdoor area. The guests were encouraged to take a box of flowers home and plant them.

A couple used their houseplants and some houseplants of friends to decorate a huge oak altar for their wedding ceremony. Baby's-breath and loose green laurel were inserted in and around the clay pots. The top of the altar was crowned with white candles.

Dried flowers can be used to make a lovely bouquet. One bride chose all-white dried flowers: lunaria, strawflowers, certain seed pods, and bleached dried ferns. There are many colorful dried flowers that could be used as well. The beauty of dried flowers is that you can keep your bridal bouquet for as long as you choose. Although this bride made her own arrangement, some florists have reported making dried bouquets for the bride and the entire wedding party.

A caterer made a thrifty suggestion for decorating a couple's small reception. They were serving food buffet style and to decorate the buffet table the caterer had the three bridesmaids lay their bouquets at the center of the table. This saved them from carrying the bouquets around and it provided fine color, minus cost, for a centerpiece.

A couple getting married in their own apartment had eight hanging baskets of flowering fuschia suspended from the ceiling. They had been purchased, via a friend, from a wholesale florist.

At a wedding in a very large cathedral, the bride and groom wanted the guests to feel warmth and welcome in the face of high-domed splendor. The ushers handed out flowers at the door to each guest. The flowers had been purchased through a street vendor at the cost of $.20 a piece. The couple bought one hundred flowers for $20. Purchasing flowers this way is useful when the date of your wedding is in the winter months and there are no garden flowers around. For $20 to $35 you can buy enough flowers from a flower stand or vendor to do bouquets and decorations for your whole wedding. Prearrange the purchase for the sake of price and available quantity. Make sure the flowers will be fresh.

Other Beautiful Ideas

Flowers aren't the only way to decorate a wedding. Here are some other ideas:

Before the ceremony, bridesmaids put burning incense in the choir loft of a church. The smell, while not overpowering, wafted an exotic feeling down through the pews of guests.

In a wedding held in an Ethical Society building, helium-filled balloons danced on the ceiling. There were about 250 balloons which the friends of the couple were responsible for discarding after the wedding. Afterward, they had a wild time—catching the balloons, popping them, and finally sweeping the floor and finishing up the reception food.

At an outdoor wedding the couple stood on an antique oriental rug that was brought to the United States in the early 1800s by a member of the groom's family. The couple will someday inherit the rug.

A wedding reception was staged around large outdoor sculptures that were moved closer together in one area of a lawn and decorated with flowers.

A home wedding adopted the Elizabethan custom of tying flowers in intervals along ribbons. White and yellow chrysanthemums were tied along yards of wide blue and yellow grosgrain.

In a large church a felt banner, made by children of the church, read CELEBRATE LIFE. Done in reds and oranges, it hung directly behind the altar.

At Arlo Guthrie's wedding, in upstate New York, a pack of puppies ran freely among the guests. The wedding took place in a meadow in the Berkshires.

The younger brothers of a bride caught a cageful of monarch butterflies which they released in the tented area of their sister's wedding reception.

There are numerous ways to use candles at a wedding. One couple was married at an evening ceremony in a church. The church had wooden candleholders which attached to the ends of each pew. The couple purchased standard white candles from a religious supply store for the pew holders and bought larger white candles for the altar. Their friends, who made sand candles, contributed several large sand candles for the surrounding stairs and front table.

Another couple wrote a candlelight ritual into their ceremony. They each lit their candle from a larger one on the altar as they spoke their vows.

At a wedding held in a park on a September evening, paper bags, filled with sand and holding lighted candles, outlined the area of the ceremony and reception.

Candleholders for pews or floor-length candlestands can be rented from some florists and all rental agencies, or they can be borrowed from a church or perhaps a theater group. Unless you have something quite specific in mind, decorations of this type are time-consuming to make.

Nevertheless, one bride did make all the hand-dipped bayberry candles for her wedding.

A canopy can be used in a situation, indoors or outdoors, where there is no designated altar area. It sets a site for the wedding vows. Canopies at weddings are an ancient custom. Jewish ceremonies have called for a *huppah* or four-postered canopy since biblical times. The origins, for Jews, go back to weddings held in tents, but today the huppah represents the new home or family sanctioned by the marriage. Traditional huppahs are usually velvet or silk with fringe and embroidery. A recent (expensive) custom of having the canopy made of fresh flowers and greens is very popular.

For Jews or non-Jews, a canopy serves as a decorative item that could be fashioned from any handsome piece of textile that the bride and groom fancy. It could be designed and made by hand by the couple, incorporating any symbols, fabrics, or colors that are significant to them. A contemporary canopy could be batiked or quilted, appliquéd, or macraméed.

Like everything else in a personalized wedding, decorations are strictly the decision of the bride and groom. You may want to go to a good deal of trouble or to no trouble at all. The decorations that you will treasure most, however, are the ones you created and executed using your own talents and the help of those who care about you.

9. CAPTURED FOREVER IN
LIVING COLOR

"What is it that you want, miss? A wedding is a wedding!"
—*Professional wedding photographer*

We weren't positive what we wanted. But we were sure that what we were looking at wasn't it. In the white and silver albums spread out before us were 8-by-10-inch color glossies which the photographer had aptly labeled "The Classics." The Classics ran something like this: bridesmaids adjusting bride's veil in someone's bedroom, everybody walking up the aisle, down the aisle, on the church steps, off the steps, couple cutting cake, couple feeding each other cake, line-ups of mothers, fathers, grandmothers (a ubiquitous flower girl appeared in *every* picture), and a peek into the back seat of the getaway car. The pictures were either staged (adjusting veil, removing garter) or they were "line-'em-up-and-shoot-'em" shots at the front of the church. We were to see "The Classics" again and again in the showrooms of myriad photographers. Indeed, from this point of view, a wedding was "just another wedding."

There were differences in price—big differences, in fact. If you're looking for a wedding photographer to do "The Classics," simply price around. In the end the less expensive photographer will give you about the same photos for about a half to a third the cost. There are all sorts of ways to calculate costs. By the picture, by the hour, by the album. The price usually ranges from $150 upward to $500 and produces a large album (for the couple to remember their "day of days") and a smaller album (for the parents to remember what it was they paid for).

Some package deals include extras such as leather-bound albums, free photo thank-you cards, and for the handsomely priced arrangements, free limousine service. The limousine service means that the driver of the limo is the photographer. According to one studio this works particularly well since the photographer can keep up with the wedding couple and presumably snap a few sparkly-eyes shots while waiting for red lights.

The wedding photographer or studio will try hard to convince you how important it is to have a portrait shot. This is usually an 11-by-14-inch, black-and-white studio shot of the bride, in her gown, looking sweet and dreamy—a kind of second First Communion. If the portrait is to be done in a studio it means a hairdo, and the wedding gown and bouquet must be brought to the photographer's before the wedding. (If you don't have the money or desire to have an extra bouquet made, the photographer will provide you with a substitute arrangement made of white plastic.) Studio portraits, needless to say, are a hassle at a time when you don't need any more hassles.

If a wedding portrait is to be taken, try to arrange to have it done at the site of the wedding before the ceremony, before the guests have arrived. Outdoor portraits of this type are becoming popular. Having a portrait shot on the day of the wedding and on location would cut down extra studio costs and might capture a "wedding day mystique" that is supposed to descend on the faces of all brides. It would definitely have the impact of being the real thing. Don't forget the groom's wedding portrait. If the bride is going to have one, so should he.

The very worst thing about formal wedding photography is that it hardly ever captures the real essence of the wedding day. There is a tremendous amount of humanity in a wedding.

There are real people interacting with people they know or love. There are honest-to-goodness preparations that go on for months or weeks in advance, culminating in a flurry on the day of the wedding. There is a locale, a day with weather, a mood.

Photography is an art form, making it very hard to define what makes a good photograph. When it comes to wedding photography, there are functions that must be fulfilled. Wedding photos are to record the events of the day. Good, unstilted wedding photos will:

1. Show the principals in action and interaction. The bride, the groom, the wedding party and families are a must for wedding pictures. Lining them up to take their pictures is probably the most deadening way to record their presence. Showing them relating to others is a much truer look.

2. Capture a feeling of the setting and the mood of the occasion. The unique or intricate details—architecture or décor —of the place the ceremony is held, the time of year, the kind of day. These are real aspects of the wedding day that can evoke real memories if captured by the photographer.

3. Show emotions. It's not easy to get human emotion on film. Those who are quick enough and astute enough to catch it are usually photojournalists, highly paid for their troubles. A wedding has moments of pure joy, tension, eagerness, reservation. An instantaneous facial gesture can be all that is visible of a strong feeling. If a photographer can capture that, he has made you a good picture.

4. Show preparation. The way wedding albums are set up it seems as if the whole thing just sprang from the instant the bridesmaids placed the veil on the bride's head. The more family and friends involved in the planning and preparation of a wedding, the more interesting it is to keep a memory of the whole event. Pictures of friends sewing, decorating, making and setting up food are better shots than friends standing still in special-occasion clothes.

How do you go about getting this kind of coverage? One way is to have your pictures taken by a friend, who knows at least a little something about photography. If you, or a friend, are taking the pictures consider the following pointers:

Use camera, film, and equipment that you are familiar with. Change your camera settings to fit the lighting wherever you are standing. If your camera is always ready to shoot, you won't miss the spur-of-the-moment shots that make memorable wedding photos.

Motorized cameras take a series of pictures from which you can choose the most expressive. When you push the shutter, the motor sends the film in front of the lens at a fast speed and the result is like movie film—only the individual shots are regular stills. Photojournalists often use this type of camera so they can catch the expression or event at its peak moment or can capture an entire action in a series of shots. Motorized cameras are expensive, but they can be rented from a camera supply store. They run through film *fast*. If you would like to have one used at your wedding, encourage the photographer to rent it before the wedding for as much time as it takes to make him or her feel comfortable with its operation. It costs about $18 to $24 a day to rent, plus the costs of lots of film and development. Of course, you get to choose from numerous photos, so the selection is a bargain. A motorized camera could be used in conjunction with another camera. It's expensive, but the "people shots" of unposed expressions and activities might be worth it to you.

Don't be afraid to use black and white. People want color because they think it's better. Color adds sometimes, but there are plenty of boring color shots. Color can add a "pat" look and detract from the composition of the picture. Black-and-white photos can be highly expressive, particularly facial shots. They hold dimensions that color flattens out. If color versus black and white is a decision you don't want to make, have two cameras covering the wedding—one in black and white.

True candid shots are those taken when the subjects are unaware of a camera. Some of the best candids can be taken at the unguarded moment right after a ritual or a planned-picture situation. At these times, someone cuts loose with a joke or a kiss while waiting for the next formal happening. If you're not totally concerned about getting shots of the main event, you can be ready for the spontaneity that follows. During receptions and other group situations, candids are at a premium, but call for "sneak" shots. Hold the camera at your side, out of view, with the strap wrapped around your arm instead of hanging from your neck. Take a reading before raising the camera, snap, and lower before rewinding. The less awareness of the camera, the more natural the photographs.

Take lots and lots of pictures. The more shots you take, the better chance of coming up with a great picture. There should be no stinting on film at a wedding celebration.

You may, nevertheless, want professional pictures as well as pictures shot by someone with a more creative bent. Parents often insist on a professional photographer and if they are willing to pay for one, why not? The photographer must not be allowed to direct the show, however. At a wedding in Pittsburgh, a very expensive photographer had his two assistants set up a box in the middle of the dance floor whereupon he rushed out and jumped up on it to snap shots of couples dancing around him. It was distracting and made everyone aware that they were on display. Other wedding photographers have a habit of pushing guests into a semicircle and snapping their pictures. Others have been known to yell "Hold it there!" and then photograph a frozen face. Extract personal assurances from whoever is doing the job that these kinds of things will not happen.

Some churches have rules about flashbulbs going off inside

the sanctuary. Some object to pictures during the actual ceremony, but allow processional and recessional shots. Other
churches bar any picture taking. Of course, you are restricted by the rules and preferences of the officiant.

If there are no such rules, you may want to lay down a few
guidelines of your own for any photographer. Nothing is
more unnerving than a photographer hiding behind a column
or potted palm or slithering on his belly near the altar to
grab a ceremony-in-progress shot. Nothing is less sacred than
a vow punctuated with an explosion of flashbulbs. There are
some places where a camera should not go. The exchange of
vows is such a personal moment that it's questionable
whether any photograph could do it dignity. It's probably
one of those instances best left to live on in the mind's eye.

Processional and recessional shots are up to you. There is
less chance of flashbulb alienation at these times. At an outdoor wedding the distraction of flashes is not a problem and
the open area makes it easier for a photographer to get shots.

To find a photographer who has real ability but isn't jaded
by a continuous diet of weddings, you might try contacting
a photography school or an art college and ask around their
photo department. Or you might call your local newspaper
and ask to talk to the photo editor. Newspaper photojournalists are pretty reliable cameramen and are notoriously
underpaid. They might welcome the money from an extra
job, especially if you tell them that your wedding is going to
be a little more interesting than average. Emphasize that you
do not want standard wedding coverage, that you're more
interested in a real, candid view of the wedding. A photographer for a large paper may have the use of a motorized
camera. He might be happy to pick up a free-lance job of
this type or he might coolly inform you that he "doesn't do
weddings." Even among their own profession, wedding
photographers are held in the lowest of esteem. Free-lance
photographers are sometimes as hungry, and you might be

able to engage the services of one whose work you like. Emphasize in all these dealings that you want a special kind of coverage.

The best photographer is someone who is skilled and who knows you. He can watch for special moments, like greeting an old friend who has come a long way to attend the wedding, kissing a favorite grandparent, or joking with a former date. He can spot friends and relatives who are interacting. If you have one or more capable friends, you can look forward to some lively pictures.

Don't be sentimental about the photographic skills of any friend or relative you ask to cover your wedding. If the person is less than talented or is not adept at working under pressure, it might be embarrassing to you both should the pictures turn out to be inadequate. There is a possible risk to a friendship in such cases. You end up really caring that it didn't work out.

The more people taking pictures, the better the selection will be. A professional photographer who has worked for years on magazines suggested that if he was having his wedding photographed, he would borrow as many inexpensive cameras (Instamatics) as he could find and pass them out at the door to every fifth guest. The cameras would be loaded and there would be a bowl of extra film sitting somewhere in the reception. Instructions would be simple—take pictures.

10. RECEPTIONS—THE END OF THE BIG BLAST

Suprême of Fresh Fruit Princess
Decorated with Blue Sugar Lovebirds
Served on Ice in Silver Cups
Tied with Pale Blue Ribbon
on Gold Doily

> Part of suggested menu in
> *The Wedding Book*

Whether you call it a reception, a party, a feast, or a celebration, the gathering after the wedding is a great occasion. As long as there are weddings there will be food-and-drink celebrations to go along with them. It's part of the happiness, close-knit warmth, and magic that find their way into weddings.

There are, of course, all kinds of traditional wedding receptions. Apart from the high kitsch of wedding palaces with their French provincial overkill, there is a pattern for the "well-done" catered affair. As a rule it takes place in a restaurant, inn, or country club, and it usually involves a cocktail hour with an enormous spread of hot and cold hors d'oeuvres, followed by dinner and dancing.

It is also well known that the cost of these affairs can run from steep to scandalous. Priced on a per head basis by the caterers, affairs of this sort can run with no trouble at all from $15 to $25 per head. Add a few extras (like a dessert table or an ice swan or two) and the per head cost escalates with ease to $50 per head and even upward.

It seems that small groups, say under thirty people, can survive this treatment and still hold a warm, cohesive party despite a regimented atmosphere. With larger groups, seating arrangements unfold, a stilted "what's next" atmosphere evolves, and the spontaneity of the celebration gets iced and set on a doily. What has happened is that the caterers' expectations have been fulfilled—you have fed heads.

Hotels and restaurants that advertise wedding plans are usually the worst. There is often an accordionist in the manager's back pocket or, worse yet, a master of ceremonies who introduces the head table and fires out directives like: "Now the bride will dance with her father." Everyone claps. All this is fairly tedious.

Wedding feasts go back to the beginnings of society in many cultures. Today they are part of being married in hundreds of countries that hold little else in common. A wedding celebration was meant to be a holiday, a release from the workaday world. Although status and wealth have always entered into the concept, it needn't be the overriding impression left by a wedding reception.

It's interesting to look at wedding traditions in the early years of this country. Settlers in pioneer America held a house-raising for newlyweds. The men would stop hammering on the house long enough to swig a little whisky, run races, hold a shooting match or a wrestling bout. A huge feast was held, either when the house was finished, or at the end of each day's building. The meal was prepared by the local women or donated by the *groom's* parents. After it was finished, someone would bring out a fiddle and there would be dancing, singing, and storytelling late into the night. The building and partying were known to go on for three days and nights.

It's a shame that the housebuilding role of today's wedding guests is no longer taken into consideration. (Rather than a roof over their heads, today's wedding guest donates an electric blender to the future well-being of the young couple.) Lost even more are the camaraderie, casualness, and sense of community that those houseraisings must have fostered.

It seems the kind of receptions most likely to come close to those rollicking days of yesterday are those now served buffet style. People have time to mingle, to meet new people, chat with old friends. They can eat at will—a posture that puts most people immediately at ease. There is more of a feeling of leisure. Buffet style works indoors and outdoors, is far cheaper than a sit-down dinner, and involves fewer people who must be hired or torn away from the festivities to serve food.

The best part of a buffet is that it needn't be catered. You and your friends can prepare food in advance, to your own tastes, at a minimal strain on the dollar. A reception you prepare yourselves with help from those who mean something to you is the most personalized reception of all.

Where to Hold a Wedding Reception

The site of your wedding reception probably will be tied closely to the site of your wedding. The only important criterion is that there be sufficient room for everyone to spread out and enjoy themselves.

If you are planning an outdoor wedding, you probably will have the food and partying on location. If your wedding is indoors, you could consider an outdoor reception according to season. You might not have to look far. A back yard, patio, or church courtyard could be the most convenient and casual reception area available. One of the nicest receptions I've attended was held in the brick and boxwood courtyard of an old, historical church. There were hardly any nontraditional elements in this wedding reception. Yet it was casual and warm, with an easy flow between church and court-yard.

Most churches are notorious for having sterile, ungainly basement rooms (known as "activity rooms") that end up housing receptions. This rule of thumb seems to run less true for large old churches where you can often find a handsome parlorlike room used for church affiliated activities. When you are choosing a church you should certainly keep these considerations in mind.

One couple found such a "receiving room" in an old stone Presbyterian church, lit it with candles, pushed the sofas and upholstered chairs closer toward the center of the room to form conversation areas and set up their stereo with favorite records. At the far end of the room was a food-ladened table.

Any beautiful room is fine for a reception. Perhaps you can rent a room or lounge in a museum, college building, or other public facility. Usually these requests can only be granted for "afterhours." One couple had a fine reception in a boat house along the Schuylkill River in Philadelphia. The boat house belonged to a rowing team who housed their sculls in the basement and maintained a woody lounge overlooking the river on the upper floor.

Or, borrow a friend's spectacular apartment or roomy house. Most friends or relatives would be flattered to lend you their home for your wedding reception.

A country home or a house at the beach or mountains would be good for a fun weekend reception. It can be borrowed or rented, but it won't work if it is too far from where the wedding is to be held. Or you can hold a general reception at the wedding site and invite anyone who can make it to join you at the reception being held at some distance.

Decorations

If you are tied in to a rather institutional-looking room,

you can decorate. The purpose of decorating is simply to brighten the place up, not to cover it with more flowers and ribbons than guests. Little time or money need be spent on this effort. Cut flowers in vases, branches of laurel or ivy tied with ribbons and baby's-breath, dried flowers, balloons or banners can liven up a reception area. Bowls of fruit and bridesmaids' bouquets on the buffet table are practical ideas. Don't bother with crepe paper and formal flower arrangements. Better bowls of confetti for everyone to throw at each other and a row of potted geraniums that guests can take home.

A very colorful reception in a church basement in Minneapolis had card tables, borrowed from friends, set up around the room with folding chairs. What saved this scene was the cotton print tablecloths that covered the card tables and the buffet table. Each cloth was a different bright print, about a yard and a half of inexpensive cotton fabric straight from the fabric store. The prints all seemed to belong together and unified what would have been a cheerless room.

At another reception held on a patio, all the food was served in baskets. Even the punch bowl was set into a large woven basket. Since the food tended to be more natural than fancy, the baskets lent just the right touch.

At a very small family reception on the side porch, all the dishes of food rested on beds of smooth, green *Hosta* leaves, cut from the back yard.

Outdoor weddings need almost no decoration. Some couples with outdoor celebrations seem to gravitate toward banners announcing that a wedding is taking place or displaying a joyful quote. If you've picked a lovely site, the decoration has been done for you.

What to Eat?

Food is entirely of your choosing. At a buffet-style wedding reception anything from hot dogs and hamburgers to *pâté* and caviar can be served and enjoyed.

Finger food works better than something that demands a plate, fork, and attention. Assorted cheeses and crackers are easy and delicious. Sometimes a cheese shop will prepare a tray of cheeses and crackers for a certain number of people. You pick up the sampler tray the day before and your reception is ready.

Dips, either with crackers, breadsticks or raw vegetables, seem to go well at buffet gatherings.

Natural finger foods are good, too. Bowls of cut fruit, nuts, raisins, and sunflower seeds can be served with freshly baked bread and honey. This, of course, if you are already a natural-foods buff.

Sandwich makings can be laid out on the table. No need for prepared sandwiches or catered fixings. The day before the wedding, raid a deli for all the cold cuts and rye bread, bagels and salads that you'll need. Some delicatessens will cater a reception, but it's really unnecessary. You can arrange cold cuts on a platter as decoratively as the deli man can. Self-made sandwiches with beer or wine or soft drinks make for a very casual, inexpensive party.

Casual can be elegant, too. One really fine reception took place in the tiny courtyard of a city townhouse on a sweltering August day. A table in the courtyard was laid out with a crisp white cloth. On the table were two large glass bowls in trays of ice. One bowl was filled with fresh-cut strawberries, grapes, cherries, peaches, and pineapple, accompanied by a small bowl of powdered sugar. The other bowl was heaped with cold, cooked shrimp alongside a bowl of cocktail sauce. Ice buckets holding champagne were on each end of the table with trays of glasses. Throughout the house, smaller bowls of fruit with powdered sugar were scattered on end tables and in conversation areas. The bowls were garnished with little bouquets of fresh mint and baby's-breath and served as decoration as well as refreshment.

Another indoor reception had four fondue pots bubbling at different points around the room. One contained cheese fondue, one beef, another seafood, and the last chocolate. At each were forks and the appropriate dunkings. All the pots had been borrowed, the eating areas covered with tablecloths, and a constant supply of sparkling burgundy was served from a table in the corner of the room. The guests (about twenty-five of them) loved it.

Picnic and cookout receptions need no explanation. An already prepared picnic might be better for a larger number of people than a cookout. Hamburgers or steak to be grilled mean that the number of guests must be small or there will be waiting involved. With the smoke, the cooking facility, presence of fire, etc., this is a more complicated way to handle an outdoor reception, though not impossible. A buffet picnic of prepared food could serve any number of people, depending on the joint effort of friends in preparation efforts.

Large or small, picnics at an outdoor reception can be highly personalized. The fare can be country French or country cousin. Deviled eggs, potato salad, and fried chicken on a gingham cloth would suit some couples while a quiche, terrine, and artichokes to nibble on would please others. The only criterion for the food is that it be prepared in advance and that there be plenty of it.

What to Drink?

Champagne, the ever-present wedding toast, probably earned its favored-drink status because nearly everybody, even non-drinkers, likes the bubbly taste. It is expensive. If you are ordering champagne, allow six or seven servings to the bottle and about three servings per guest. That translates to about a bottle for every two people present. If this doesn't scare you off, purchase the champagne by the case. Some stores give you a discount on case purchases and will lend you the champagne glasses you need free of charge. Glasses may also be rented from a rental agency at ten to fifteen cents apiece. Clear-plastic, disposable stemware is widely available and would cost less per glass. It seems more sensible for outdoor weddings.

Outdoors, or with limited refrigerator space, you could keep champagne cool as you would any other drink. Buy a new plastic trash can or Styrofoam cooler, maybe decorate it, and fill with ice. Pack in the champagne bottles.

The cost of a reception for seventy-five people could be cut by $75 if champagne punch is served rather than straight champagne.

Other punches are just as reasonable. Wine punches are light and inexpensive while punches with liquor are more expensive and pack a suprising per-cup wallop. (One bride and groom, with a punch bowl at their reception, did the ladling out themselves. That way they got to greet everyone and were a central part of the celebration while still helping out.)

Sherry is a good drink for a wedding reception. It costs far less than champagne. You can buy a half gallon of respectable domestic sherry for under $5.00.

Sangria, easily homemade, is great for weddings, too.

Japanese plum wine was served at one wedding—both the red and white varieties. This is a sweet, sensitive wine, rather unique and somehow just right for a certain type of wedding reception. It's not cheap. Buy a bottle and see what you think.

Of course, any wine that you and your friends enjoy, foreign or domestic, belongs at a celebration designed for your enjoyment.

Although it is a personal prejudice, I feel that hard liquor at a wedding reception doesn't work as well as some of the drinks mentioned above.

Liquor is quite expensive and when bought to stock a bar for mixed drinks becomes even more expensive since you need a complete variety on hand. It's hard to see how you could purchase liquor, mixers, and garnishes for a reception of fifty for much under $100. This would include ingredients for only the most common mixed beverages. If a bartender were hired to free-lance the occasion, the cost would double.

If everyone is going to get high, it seems far more festive to get high on a "celebration" drink like champagne or sangria than on a succession of mixed potions like scotch and water. But again, that's how I feel about it.

For many guests, particularly older and middle-aged ones, mixed drinks are a sign of hospitality and graciousness. At a buffet-style reception you could have a bar as easily as a table with punch. If you do choose to include a bar, let one person be responsible for stocking, setting up, and manning it during the reception. Perhaps a friend or relative would be willing to take on this duty as a wedding gift.

Or, you might prefer to hire a bartender to free-lance the occasion. Some bartenders work through referral by a caterer; some can be contacted through mixology schools in larger cities. The cost will vary greatly, depending on what your needs are and the size of the wedding. Most free-lance bartenders work only under specific conditions agreed on beforehand to prevent themselves from being overworked at the reception. Most expect a tip in addition to their fee.

Logistics

Who prepares a wedding reception if there is no caterer involved? You do. With the help of your family and/or friends. It all starts out with a planning session. Most couples would like a casual atmosphere, while not leaving the whole affair to potluck. Plan what kind of foods you want, when you will make them, how much to make, and the cost. Many heads are better than two on this kind of planning.

Time is an important factor. You need plenty of it. Whipping up potato salad for fifty is more time-consuming than you may imagine. Make in advance anything that can be frozen, and freeze it. This includes most baked goods. Avoid dishes that must be prepared on the day of serving. To have everything ready on the day before the wedding, chop, cook, or blend whatever can be made ahead of time in the two- or three-day period before. Borrow friends' or neighbors' refrigerators to house prepared food. The day of final preparation is the day before the wedding. On the wedding day itself the only kitchen work that should be attempted is the reheating of previously prepared food.

It may be that you would prefer to stop at the planning stage and leave the execution to friends and family. This is entirely reasonable. You'll have plenty of odds and ends to keep up with during the time the food preparation is going · on. To attempt to do everything is to put a strain on yourselves and rob you of some of the enjoyment of the wedding itself. Ask trusted friends and competent family members to help. Then leave it up to them.

For a wedding present, the sister of one bride produced an imaginative French-cuisine buffet, mostly prepared in advance and served in the family's living room after the wedding. It was a magnificent present. Since the sister was a cook in a French restaurant, it was within her realm to donate such a gift.

At several weddings, the wedding party took the food on as its responsibility. Since the members weren't burdened down with renting tuxes or attending rehearsal affairs, they had the time and resources to put together a party. In both cases a casual buffet party resulted.

If any paid help is needed, it might be at serving time. No one really wants to be behind an apron full time, when the rest of the party is flowing along. Mothers responsible for receptions would find themselves hoofing glasses and refilling serving bowls if there was no one else doing it. In fact, this is one of the main reasons caterers are hired in the first place, less for their food than to free people from having to serve or prepare the food.

If you feel it is necessary to leave everyone free to have a good time, you can easily hire non-professional help. Neighborhood teen-agers, college students, or older women might be interested in this type of employment. Your parents might have inroads to a PTA or church group who would help keep things rolling at the reception for a donation to their organization.

Invite whoever is in charge to come over ahead of time and explain where everything will be. Make a list of what needs to be done during the ceremony and a diagram of how things are to be laid out. Explain all. Then sit back, trust, and let events take their course. If everything runs smoothly, fine. If not, it's fine too. You are not aiming for perfection—just a good time. Even if mistakes occur, they're quickly forgotten during a happy party with friends.

Hiring help probably wouldn't be necessary for very small receptions. At a small buffet, food can be laid out and people can come and get it as they choose. Serving bowls don't empty quite so quickly.

Renting Sundries

There are rental agencies to help you amass a large amount of any party-type commodity that you need. They may be helpful. For instance, if you could use a 72-cup percolator, you either need a good friend at the PTA or Fire Department or you need to rent it. You can—for about $6.00 a day.

For $.25 to $.45 apiece you can rent metal folding chairs.

Older people are not comfortable sitting on floors, the ground, or large rocks.

You can rent a huge punch bowl if you need one, though several small punch bowls would be friendlier, and you could usually borrow those.

If you're a debutante type, or would like to be, you can rent a striped tent with lighting and dance floor for a neat $500 to $800.

However, it is possible to borrow these items (except for the tent) from friends, friends of friends, and neighbors. Everything does not have to match. Really. In the end no one at a buffet or picnic is going to remember what kind of glasses and napkins you presented.

Rental agencies close their doors behind you and try to scare you into renting all sorts of extras: silver candelabras and vinyl-padded portable bars. One rental agency put out a list entitled "36 Things You Dare Not Forget for Your Wedding Reception." The first dare-not on the list: a champagne fountain.

In the end, chairs, long buffet tables, and large kitchen equipment seem to be the most unobtainable items. Silverware can be borrowed as can tablecloths, large serving bowls, and other serving implements. For large crowds, paper plates and napkins and plastic glasses make sense unless they offend your ecological standards. In which case, you do the dishes. And that brings us to:

Cleaning Up

If you are not employing a caterer, cleaning up the site of the reception is your responsibility. It is particularly important if you are using a public park, a friend's home, etc. Sometimes you could arrange for clean-up the next day, but most of the time you would have to clean up the reception area immediately following the reception.

Usually the best group of people to ask for help in cleaning up are those friends who were in your wedding party. They were chosen as special people to represent you in the ceremony itself and will probably not feel put-out at being asked to clean up. They may, or may not, be the same people responsible for preparing the food. Those who brought food can be counted on (or maybe asked) to help clean up, too.

If you yourselves stay to clean up, there are bound to be some people to lend a hand. The whole clean-up procedure can be as fun an experience as the party itself.

Or, you might want to instigate a small afterparty get-together of special friends from the reception. Making clean-up an exclusive activity will help gather a pleased crew.

Wedding Cake

It used to be that the white tiered wedding cake was sacred. Wedding styles could come and go, but the white tiered wedding cake was considered part of society's civilized nature. Though they are by no means extinct, the white tiered wedding tower—especially the kind with the plastic bride and groom on top—are showing new form and spirit. Sometimes the change is interior. The white icing may be covering up a chocolate or chocolate-chip cake, layered with raspberry filling or ice cream. But more often the whole cake has changed into whatever tickles the fancy and sweet tooth of the couple.

Any color icing or decoration goes. At an otherwise strictly traditional Italian wedding, the bride had insisted on rum cake iced in bright red. A gay pink cake with orange trim sported a top bouquet of orange lilies at a church wedding. A heart-shaped cake, iced in pink, showed up at another church affair.

Occasionally there is a surprise on the bride and groom. When a couple who had been living together for a number of years decided to marry, the parents of the bride asked to be allowed to order the cake. They did—a large, white tiered regular, with FINALLY! scrawled on top in yellow icing.

If you are going to buy a wedding cake and want the cake to be personalized, keep in mind that you are within your rights. Find a baker who will agree to your specifications.

You might find a departure from the run-of-the-mill bakery cake, which is often dry cake covered with supersweet, smeary icing, by experimenting with a few ethnic bakeries. An Italian, Swiss, or German pastry shop may give you a delicious new alternative to the American bakery cake. Europeans, unlike Americans, have never been afraid to season their cakes with liquor, making for zippier tastes and richer texture. Gourmet shops, while not selling the type of cake you're looking for, usually know of some fine local cook who caters and would be able to do justice to a made-to-order cake.

One couple who married at Christmas time had a classic French Noël log baked for them by a small, elegant restaurant that was one of their favorite eating places. The cake was more expensive than one purchased from a bakery. But it was unique, beautiful, and entirely delicious.

Although a wedding cake is not a major expense, it is something that you might want to make on your own or have made by a loving volunteer.

In one rare instance, the neighbor of the groom's grandmother(!) had enjoyed a great deal of success at cake-decorating courses she was taking at the local adult night school. While not even invited to the wedding, she donated a large cake that was covered from top to bottom with flowers, animals, baskets, bells, candles, etc. The cake was so painstakingly baroque that it became the conversation piece at this small reception and was carefully examined before a single piece was cut.

If you, or a friend, are going to make the cake, be advised that it involves a certain amount of trouble. You can find a recipe that allows you to use packaged cake mixes or you can start from scratch. The start-from-scratch recipes abound in the cookbooks of our land.

If you are making your own, you might consider two large layer cakes or a large square-pan cake. Both of these options would be easier to construct, ice, and cut than a tiered cake. One mother of the bride made two large cakes in angel food pans from a recipe that added instant-pudding mix, oil, and a few other extra moistening ingredients to a regular cake mix. The cakes were turned out, iced with white frosting, and covered with shredded coconut. A small nosegay of flowers was inserted inside the center hole of each cake.

You can bake layers ahead of time, freeze them immediately in aluminum foil wrapping, and defrost and decorate the day before the wedding. Cake, however, shouldn't be frozen for longer than three weeks before it is to be used. Icing doesn't freeze well at all.

Of course, no one says that you *must* have a wedding cake. There are alternatives. At a true bacon-and-eggs wedding breakfast, cherry danish pastries were served rather than cake. A picnic wedding offered a large basket, decorated with ribbons and filled with pink- and yellow-frosted cupcakes. You could have cheesecake with a choice of fruit toppings, or a pile of scrumptious-looking French or Italian pastries.

In some areas it is the custom for the bride and groom to freeze the top tier of their wedding cake, to be brought out and enjoyed on the first anniversary. This happened to the pink-and-orange wedding cake mentioned earlier. The couple froze the small top tier and when their first anniversary rolled around they took it with them to share with a faraway friend who had been unable to make it to the wedding.

The Officiant at the Reception

At outdoor weddings and weddings where the officiant is a friend of the couple, there is no question that he will stay for the reception. This is not always so at church weddings. Invite the officiant to the reception. If he chooses not to come, don't be insulted or feel rejected. Several ministers and priests I talked to expressed an opinion summed up by this quote from one clergyman: "I don't go to receptions. It's a personal thing, but I don't feel I belong there. My role has been such that I can't enjoy them. People ask me all the same questions, talk about the wedding, expect standard answers from me in response to their standard questions. I do forty or so weddings a year and in my long history of weddings I've found that there's no comfortable place for the minister at the reception."

11. MIXED BLESSINGS

There are so many matters to think about and things to look forward to during the time you plan for a wedding. Overseeing the handling of wedding presents is a time-consuming part of wedding detail. Simultaneously mapping out plans for a honeymoon makes the list of items and events to coordinate even longer. The gifts and the honeymoon are part of the traditional aura of wedding excitement. They can be real fun. And yet . . .

The Gift-Horse Stampede

Setting up a household is a major part of the wedding-household-honeymoon stretch mentioned in the beginning of this book. If you have ever picked up an issue of *Brides* magazine, or seen a table loaded with gifts at a wedding reception, you need not be convinced that gift giving is still an overwhelming part of all traditional and most non-traditional weddings.

What you may not be convinced of is your own need for an automatic toaster-oven, teakwood free-form ice bucket, or, even more removed, your very own china and silver patterns.

Many young couples are living extended single lives, setting up their own households with furnishings not intended to be serving interim time until married life comes to the rescue. They have a fairly complete household in existence. Should they move in with their intended, as a majority now do, there is an overabundance to cope with.

For example, Sarah had been out of college and living alone for four years when she met Chris. He'd been doing nicely on his own for five years. Since they lived in the suburbs on polar sides of New York City, they decided rather quickly to move in together so they could avoid the commute necessary to see each other. Neither apartment was large enough to house the results of a combined nine years of salaried single life. The resulting move was like Noah's ark: There were two of everything. Two coffee pots, two stereo sets, two sofas, two beds. Not to mention one prized antique dining room table versus one handsome, large butcher-block-and-chrome dining table. For certain, they didn't need wedding presents.

Josie and Ray met in a graduate school program and planned a wedding to follow graduation. They had little regard or love for material things. Both wanted to travel across country as soon as they graduated. They contemplated buying a farm in Nova Scotia after that. Their apartment was a collection of posters and pillows and cinder-block bookshelves. What they didn't want was a collection of wedding presents.

Carol and Bob were married in a personalized, but rather traditional, fashion. They didn't have a wealth of household goods but looked forward to accumulating comfortable, appreciated possessions over a period of time. They had a yen for plants, crafts, and antiques. They didn't want closetsful of trays, appliances, or casserole sets that they would seldom use and never love.

How can it be that a guest will eagerly give a lovely Lenox candy dish to a couple married in flowers and freedom at the local park? It's true. That happened. Silver butter dishes are still wrapped in white-and-silver paper and mindlessly rushed off at the first sign of a wedding.

Of course, commercial interests help. The ads for sterling, silver, china, crystalware, and other important sundries are militant. The bridal industry has wedding guests brainwashed as well. There are certain wedding gifts that like it or not, you can expect to receive as presents.

Individualized Gifts—to Ask for and Give

If, like many other couples, you find gifts of that sort to be useless, there are alternatives. It may seem crass to list gifts to ask for as wedding presents, but many people do ask you what you want when you are preparing to be married. If they don't ask you, they'll ask your parents or friends. Should the return to their query be shrugged shoulders, or a "don't get us anything" response, you can be sure you'll receive a safe gift. A safe gift is approved for gift giving at weddings. It may be that safe gifts, like six matching engraved ashtrays, are just what you always didn't want. The giver has disappointed you while trying to please you. You write a fake thank-you note and file the gift away in the closet—or worse.

Following is a list taken from a poll of young married and about-to-be married couples as to gifts that they would like to have that could be given as wedding presents. Some are cheap, some are expensive—just like "approved" gifts. They're listed here for your consideration as to requesting or giving.

A photograph of the couple, before, during, or after the wedding, enlarged and framed

A birdfeeder with seed, or a plant holder

An old, or handmade, quilt

Garden tools or hand tools—hammer, drill, saw

Adult board games or skill games to enjoy on rainy evenings

A gift certificate for gourmet shop, cheese shop, or health-food store

An ice-cream maker

A set of good, sharp knives with utility handles

An art wall calendar

A hammock—either the Ecuadorian kind of woven threads or a simple Army-Navy variety decorated personally for the couple

Magazine subscriptions—perhaps to unique publications such as *The Smithsonian, National Wildlife,* or the English version of *Réalités*

Reference books—dictionary, atlas, thesaurus

Any beautiful book

Houseplants—the larger kind that one would be less likely to splurge on

Experience gifts—season tickets to a series of concerts, plays, films, or sports events; skin-diving lessons for two; membership in indoor tennis courts or swimming pool; a membership for a museum or for the Sierra Club

A sampler set of liqueurs or a wine rack filled with favorite wines

Sports items—a pair of bicycles(!), toboggan, sleeping bags

Educational gifts—double or individual tuition to a course at a college, cooking class, foreign language lessons, exercise class, yoga lessons

Something old—an antique chair, clock, vase, or any item, big or small, that is unique and beautiful

A work of art—a print, etching, sculpture, or painting

A craft—a piece of pottery, weaving, wall hanging, glass

And last but far from least—Cash. According to many young couples, cold cash is cool. Cash from weddings was usually spent on rather down-to-earth necessities—apartment security deposit, down payment on a car, moving expenses. Cash wedding presents were remembered, and appreciated. One couple said they didn't like the depersonalized aspect of cash—its anonymity. But most people agreed that it came in quite handy.

Altruistic Gifts

A couple in Oregon enclosed a note with each wedding invitation requesting that gifts to the bride and groom be withheld. Well-wishers were asked to give time or money to an organization bettering man and his environment. Money was sent all over the world in their behalf to a variety of worthy causes, from orphans to wildlife. A magnanimous idea.

No Gifts

One couple wanted no wedding presents. They did not need the presents and did not want to promote the commercialization of their marriage. They stated this decision by a brief "No gifts, please" on the bottom of the invitation. Their decision was firm, clear, and accepted without question.

Returning Gifts for Fun and Profit

Once you have before you all the wedding gifts, weed those out you don't like, can't use, or have six copies of and take them promptly back to the stores from whence they came. It's usually fairly uncomfortable to ask a giver of a wedding present where it came from when you plan to return it. Sometimes there is an easy clue on the label or box or accompanying card. If no clue, leave the gift wrappings attached and take it back to a department store. Chances are they'll accept it if they think there is any likelihood that it was purchased at their establishment. You'll, of course, assure them that there is every likelihood. Many people don't realize that you don't have to have a receipt to return a present that has been given to you.

This isn't rude. It's sane. Returning what you can't use to replace it with something you love and need is sensible. You may or may not choose to inform the giver of your decision. Unfortunately, in these kinds of situations, honesty works well about half the time and discretion the remaining half.

One couple I know, without scruples, returned eight place settings of "Royal Danish" sterling, plus a number of silver trays, pitchers, and salad sets. The very same day they purchased a quadrophonic stereo receiver and two extra speakers. They claim that no one (until now) was the wiser.

Thank-You Notes

Thank-you notes are nice. They needn't be stilted or gooey. You can deliver a thank-you over the phone or in person that will suffice just as well.

If a gift is so unbearable that you cannot write a thank-you note in good conscience, then don't write one. Or, thank the person for coming to your wedding or, perhaps, for "remembering."

The only really rude thank-you-note procedures are little cards with the couple's picture printed on them and a pre-printed line or two, i.e., "Charlie and Cheryl thank you for your lovely gift." This *is* cold.

If you do write thank-you notes, know that the bride is not stuck with writing them all anymore. Literate grooms write half the batch nowadays.

Some good advice the etiquette books do have to offer is

the idea that doing thank-you notes as gifts come in is a totally superior method to doing them all at once—a bleary-eyed task.

A *Really Bad Idea*

Gift tables set up to display the couple's accumulated wedding gifts. For some reason Emily Post and cohorts approve this gesture which is nevertheless deeply rooted in the heritage of bad taste. It is strictly status-conscious, competitive consumerism.

The Honeymoon Is Over

According to bridal industry economic research, the "average" honeymoon in the United States lasts 8.2 days and costs $597. It is the final leg of the three-way wedding stretch and might logically be the first link to mass change in that triad of hysteria. The honeymoon might be amended or eliminated because its function has disappeared.

The idea of a honeymoon, as known to everyone, was to permit the couples to become sexually acquainted. Implicitly, it was a period when the groom could deflower the blushing bride in private.

Recent sexual mores have made this a dated concept to say the least.

Almost all couples agree that it is great to take a vacation together. Many of them feel that immediately following their wedding celebration is not the time to do it.

As Sarah says: "There were all our friends from great distances. People we hadn't seen since college. Everyone was having a great time and we wanted to talk to them all. A bunch of us went back to our apartment after the reception was over." Chris agrees: "We were going to go away but we canceled our plans on the spot. It was so good to see everybody. Sarah met some of my finest friends. We sat around and drank and smoked and opened wedding gifts. It doesn't sound particularly exciting, but it was great."

They took a two-week vacation later in that month. But they wouldn't call it a honeymoon.

A couple from Pennsylvania was planning to spend the weekend after their wedding at a New Jersey beach resort. They were rained out. They spent the weekend in their own city, spending the resort money on delicious dinners at restaurants they had always wanted to try.

One couple, married in August, backpacked out to Cape Hatteras on the North Carolina coast.

Another, married in a mountain meadow in Oregon, spent the night in an old inn near the site of their wedding.

Oftentimes the evenings following a personalized wedding are spent with friends, at parties, cleaning up after the reception, or in some other unplanned, unforced situation.

You can take a trip after your wedding if you have the funds and the inclination to do so. It might be really fun. The timing might be just right.

The point is you don't have to. You might be just as happy enjoying the glow of being newly married in the privacy of your own environment.